The New Complete Coffee Book

THE NEW COMPLETE COFFEE BOOK

a gourmet guide to buying, brewing, and cooking

completely revised and expanded

by sara perry

photographs by maron caruso

CHRONICLE BOOKS

SAN FRANCISCO

Library of Congress Cataloging-in-Publication Data:

Perry, Sara.

The new complete coffee book :

a gourmet guide to buying, brewing,

and cooking

by Sara Perry; photographs by Maren Caruso.

    p. cm.

Includes index.

ISBN 0-8118-4021-2 (pbk.)

1. Coffee. 2. Cookery (Coffee). I. Title.

TX817.C6 P4724 2001

641.6'373—dc21

Printed in China

Composition by Suzanne Scott

Prop styling by Carol Hacker

Food styling by Diane Gsell

The photographer wishes to thank Steps of Rome,

Caffe Roma, Peaberry's Coffee and Tea, Graffeo,

Caffe Malvina, and McLaughlin Coffee Company, Inc.

Distributed in Canada by Raincoast Books

9050 Shaughnessy Street

Vancouver, BC V6P 6E5

10 9 8 7 6 5 4 3 2

Chronicle Books LLC

85 Second Street

San Francisco, California 94105

www.chroniclebooks.com

To Pete, my favorite coffee companion.

And to Matthew, Julie, Brian, Dylan, and Sofia,
who have proved to be as stimulating as caffeine.

acknowledgments

Thanks go to the friends who generously shared their ideas, time, and recipes, especially Jerry Baldwin, Kathlyn and Matthew Meskel, Mandy Groom, Joann Vazquez, Thomas Bruner, Bob and Barbara Weisman, Larry Kirkland, Jim Roberts, Karen Brooks, Bette Sinclair, Ron Paul, and Starbucks' Martha Nielsen. To Peet's Coffee and Tea, which provided a delicious array of beans for recipe testing. To Brasserie Montmartre for its enthusiatic support of my after-dinner coffee drink testing. And to Catherine Glass, whose confidence and advice are always invaluable.

Finally, as always, my thanks go to Bill LeBlond, senior editor at Chronicle Books, for his trust, patience, and friendship.

contents

introduction

When I was six, my mother's best friend, Gracie, came to visit us in Los Angeles and I was allowed to open a bright red tin of Hills Bros. Coffee. I knew it must be something good. On the outside of the can was an exotic-looking man in a flowing yellow robe and white turban, sipping a mysterious drink. The whoosh of aroma as I opened the lid told me that this was something I had to try. Holding a china cup brimming with hot milk, sugar, and a touch of black coffee, and listening to my mother and Gracie talk, I experienced for the first time a pleasure that you and I savor: coffee and conversation.

For those of you coming to *The Complete Coffee Book* for the first time, this revised edition offers you all the sterling principles for brewing a terrific cup of coffee, plus marvelous recipes featuring coffee. For those of you who own the first edition, here you'll find updated information on brewing methods, plus dozens of new recipes, including a sensuous mole, a divinely devilish mocha meringue dessert, a simple and elegant Italian morning cake, and an out-of-this-world tiramisù.

Along with beverages to enjoy with a friend on a hot summer's day, such as iced coffee, an old-fashioned soda, and an espresso milkshake, this edition has a new section of recipes for favorite adult coffee drinks. The classics are here, like Irish Coffee and Coffee Nudge, laced with flavorful liqueurs and spirits, as well as some inspirational drinks like Monastery and Coffee Cloud.

Coffee has long been one of life's subtle pleasures; few beverages are as satisfying, comforting, or stimulating. So, follow me through the history of the cup and watch the modest bean as it changes from cherry to brew. Learn to distinguish once and for all among confusing coffee labels that make choosing coffee a chore. Discover the fine points of brewing, and treat yourself to the Resources guide, which lists coffee retailers, books, and informative Web sites. I hope that this book will help you capture the split-second, stop-action pleasure that comes with that first sip of coffee, that first taste of bean

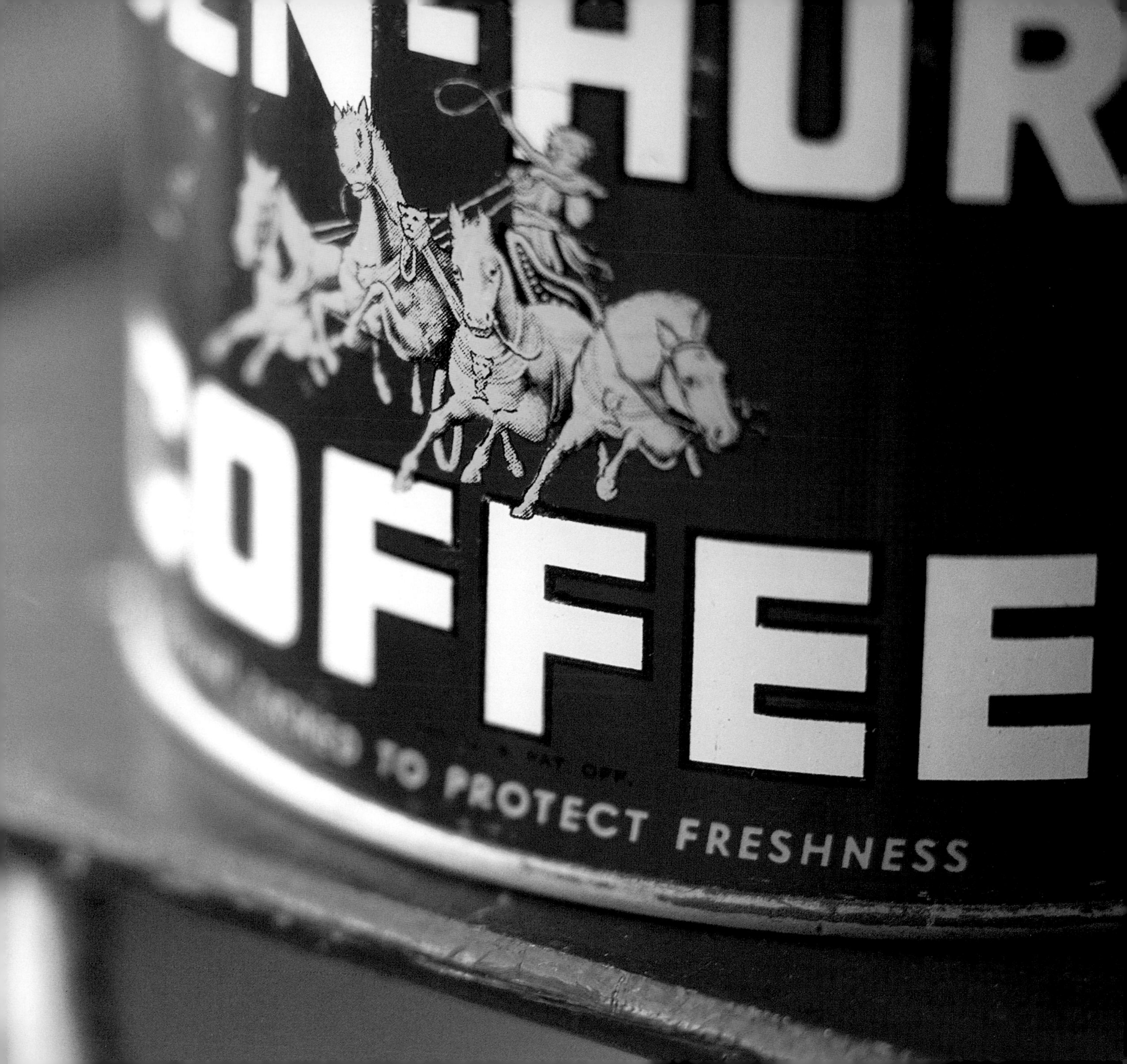
COFFEE
PAT. OFF.
TO PROTECT FRESHNESS

the history

Coffee's origins are lost in legend, but a frequently told story attributes the discovery to a sixth-century herd of tired, hungry goats and their Ethiopian caretaker, Kaldi. Weary of searching for greener pastures and eager to eat, Kaldi's herd resorted to nibbling the sweet red berries from strange bushes. Unusual behavior soon followed. Old billy goats began to kick up their heels with an exuberance that the prancing nannies found quite appealing. Witnessing this lively behavior, Kaldi decided to try the berries too, and soon he was cavorting across the hillside. When he confided his discovery of the divine berries to a monk, the news was heralded at the nearby monastery. Evening prayers suddenly became more pleasant, and the glories of the heavenly berries spread.

Until the tenth century, coffee was considered a food. Ethiopian tribesmen mixed the wild berries with animal fat, rolled the mixture into balls, and ate them during their nomadic journeys. Later, they crushed the berries and fermented them into wine. By the thirteenth century, coffee's restorative powers were well documented in the Islamic world. It was considered a potent medicine, as well as a religious potion that helped to keep the faithful awake during lengthy prayers. Islamic pilgrims spread coffee's virtues throughout the Middle East, and by the end of the fifteenth century, coffeehouses had supplanted neighborhood mosques as favorite meeting places.

To maintain tight control over their profitable coffee trade, Arab traders sold only boiled or roasted beans. Coffee beans that could germinate and grow into fruit-bearing coffee plants were not allowed out of Arabia. It was not until the early seventeenth century that a Moslem pilgrim smuggled the first fertile beans into India. Baba Budan was reputedly the fellow who snatched seven seeds and tied them around his waist on his holy pilgrimage to Mecca. When he returned home, he planted the seeds and nurtured the prolific bushes. The enterprising Dutch soon arrived at his doorstep and convinced him to part with some of his young trees, and within a few years dozens of countries were cultivating coffee's supreme beans.

Venetian traders were the first to bring Arabian beans to Europe. The Christian world was skeptical about the pagan brew, and Pope Clement VII decided that it required papal review. After one sip, his Holiness knew that this drink was worthy of confirmation. Sanctified, coffee no longer required an apothecary's prescription. Instead, it became the social beverage of Europe's middle class and was hawked alongside lemonade on street corners.

In 1637, the first European coffeehouse opened in England, and within thirty years coffeehouses had replaced taverns as the island's social, commercial, and political melting pots. Known as "penny universities," they were places where any subject might be discussed for the price of a cup of coffee. Men with similar interests frequented specific establishments. As a result, a number of newspapers, banks, and insurance houses sprang to life around the crowded wooden tables and among the heady aromas of roasted beans. Lloyd's of London, the famous insurance company, began at Edward Lloyd's coffeehouse, a place where sea merchants and underwriters gathered to talk and do business.

please tip the waiters

Conspicuously placed in London coffeehouses, brass boxes etched with the inscription "To Insure Promptness" encouraged customers to pay for efficient service. The resulting acronym, TIP, has become a byword.

how much for a pound?

In 1683, William Penn, the founder of Pennsylvania, purchased a pound of coffee in New York for $4.68. In 2000, a pound of Peet's Major Dickason's Blend sold on the Internet for $11.45.

As the seventeenth century's haven for male networking, English coffeehouses excluded females. In 1674, some unhappy wives published *A Women's Petition Against Coffee*, declaring that it was unhealthy for men to be spending so much time away from their homes. A year later, King Charles II tried to shut down the establishments, but he was unsuccessful, and for the next quarter century English coffeehouses continued to be male bastions. Then, during the eighteenth century, the middle class began moving back into neighborhood taverns, and London coffeehouses evolved into select clubs. Tea became a popular beverage not only at Court but among commoners, because it was a drink women and men could enjoy together.

Coffeehouses declined in England, but they continued to be popular gathering places throughout Italy, Germany, France, and other European countries. One favorite Parisian haunt was the Café Procope, which opened its doors as a coffeehouse in 1689 and over the years welcomed philosophers such as Rousseau and Voltaire (who purportedly consumed forty cups of coffee each day). Today, Café Procope remains a lively meeting place.

Tea was the beverage of choice for most American colonists until Boston threw its great tea party. The Dutch had introduced coffee in 1660 and served it in coffeehouses fashioned after the English model. These became the rendezvous for revolutionary activities against King George of England and his tea tax, where customers such as John Adams and Paul Revere brewed a potent cup of coffee and politics. The boycott of tea, the Boston Tea Party in 1773, and the fight for freedom established coffee as the traditional democratic drink of Americans.

the bean

Your coffee's rich, dark brew begins with the coffee tree's fruit, also called a "cherry." Resembling a cranberry in size and shape, the red, fully ripe cherry has a sweet pulp and two flat-sided green seeds or beans. These beans are protected by a parchmentlike husk and a silky, opaque chaff, called the silverskin. (When only one concave bean develops inside the cherry, it is called a peaberry.)

Most plants bloom first, then bear fruit. The small, shrublike evergreen coffee tree does both at once, blooming with jasmine-scented white flowers at the same time that it bears ripe and unripe fruit. This natural quirk makes growing and harvesting coffee extremely labor-intensive, because the ripe beans must be picked selectively.

An average healthy coffee tree produces five pounds of green beans a year, or about 2,000 beans. Of these, perhaps 400 beans are top quality, plucked over the course of a season with painstaking care. Each time you savor a shot of espresso, you're enjoying the essence of 60 beans. So, about a week's worth of espresso equals a season's worth of beans. Thought-provoking, don't you think?

Although there are many species of coffee trees, only one produces exceptional coffee. *Coffea arabica* (pronounced a-*rab*-ica), which was first found growing in Yemen centuries ago, is the sole producer of quality beans. The most widely cultivated coffee plant, it accounts for 70 percent of the world's production. Arabica thrives at higher altitudes — between 3,000 and 6,000 feet — where its beans mature slowly and have time to develop body and density. At these heights, the beans may take six or seven months to ripen, but the slower rate of fruit maturation gives them more time to develop flavor.

Coffea canephura var. *robusta* is the type you are most likely to drink when you follow instructions to "add hot water and stir." Discovered in Africa toward the end of the nineteenth century, robusta is relatively new to the coffee industry but its role is significant. Because of its hardiness, high yield, and ability to grow at lower altitudes, its beans are cheaper to produce. This makes them ideal for blending with arabicas and for use in instant coffee. For those who crave caffeine more than flavor, robustas have twice the kick of arabicas.

Coffee trees do best in tropical and subtropical climates. They will die if the temperature dips below freezing. The trees will grow in almost any soil, but they thrive in areas rich with volcanic minerals. In the seventeenth century, wild coffee trees from the highlands of Ethiopia were transported to the tropics. Today, they flourish as cultivated plants. The rainy season nurtures their growth, the sun ripens their fruit, and their beans mature in two to three months at these lower altitudes.

Depending on the type of coffee you drink, where the beans were grown, and the climatic conditions, your beans will have been harvested in one of two ways. The first is strip harvesting, the method used to harvest robustas. Either by hand or machine, the cherries (and other tree debris) are

tasting terminology

Acidity is the sharp, snappy taste that sparks the flavor of coffee. It has nothing to do with bitter, unpleasant sensations or your coffee's pH. Coffee's acids develop as the bean is roasted. They are prominent in lighter roasts but are destroyed in darker ones.

Aroma refers to the fragrance of a coffee. Your nose, the first judge of the flavors released from the bean, will tell you a great deal about your coffee's freshness and personality.

Body is the heaviness and thickness of coffee as it touches your tongue. Remember how a hearty red wine slides down your throat, while a white wine seems to glide? In the same way, a rich Sumatran and a mild Mexican coffee give you different weight sensations. You'll notice that coffee made using a paper filter has less body than coffee made using a metal filter, as in the espresso or plunger pot method.

Flavor is a combination of acidity, aroma, and body. Defining it is a little like trying to define love. It's all in the relationship. In some cases, one quality stands out, for instance, the singular tang of a Costa Rican. In others, like a full-flavored Sumatran, a broader range of qualities is celebrated.

shaken or stripped from the branches onto sheets laid under each tree. Pickers sift through the downfall with large metal screens to collect the cherries, which are then ready for the initial sorting and processing.

The second, and more costly, method is to handpick the cherries. All arabica beans are handpicked. It is a slow and meticulous job finding the ripe cherry clusters hidden among the foliage. And since arabicas grow in mountainous areas, the ground is not level, making it all the more difficult to stand and pick.

As soon as the cherries are removed from the trees, their sweet pulp begins to ferment. To remove the pulp and prepare the beans for roasting, growers process them using one of two methods. The dry method, which is cheaper, is used almost exclusively for robusta beans, and the wet method is used for arabicas.

The *dry method* is the oldest and most natural manner of processing coffee beans. The fruit is spread out to dry and shrivel in the sun. Workers rake the cherries several times during a three- to four-week period to make sure they dry evenly. After being put through a milling machine to separate out the dirt and debris, the beans are graded, bagged, and shipped to roasters. In areas where water is scarce, this method is also used for high-quality coffees such as Ethiopian Harrars and the coffees of Yemen.

The *wet method* is used with handpicked quality beans. The cherries are placed in water, and the overripe and damaged ones rise to the top. The others are channeled into a machine that bruises the skins. The water is drained, and the beans rest in tubs or tanks for up to two days, where the pulp begins to decompose. Knowing the right moment to wash off the fermenting pulp takes skill. If fermentation goes on too long, the beans develop an aftertaste and their value plummets. After the pulp is removed, the beans are dried in the open or in commercial tumble dryers. Finally, a hulling machine removes the protective parchment, and men and women patiently grade the beans by size, shape, and quality; pack them in 60-kilogram (approximately 132-pound) bags; and ship them to roasters around the world. (The remaining silverskin flecks off during roasting.) While electronic sorting is making inroads, many still consider the human eye the best judge of coffee beans.

By the time the beans reach the importer or roaster, they have passed many inspections, but there is one final test that is crucial. It is called *cupping*. High tech be damned — this is a meeting between man and bean. This is when a professional taster, or "cupper," evaluates the quality and value of a bean with equipment that resembles that of an old-fashioned chemist's lab. A sample of beans is given a light roast, and with a tasting technique that rivals tea and wine judgings, the beans are evaluated. *Ashy, earthy, nutty, bitter, salty, sour* — the list of adjectives used to describe them contains over 500 words. With these terms, the cuppers can let potential roasters know what to expect from the beans they are buying. The long journey, from tree to thee, is almost complete.

name your bean

When you buy coffee, you are confronted with exotic names that indicate either the country of origin or how long the bean was roasted.

Arabica beans are identified by their geographical origin. Pure and unblended, they possess the characteristic flavor and aroma of their native soil. Further geographical appellations name the district, plantation, or port from which the beans were shipped. A coffee labeled Ethiopian Harrar tells you that the beans were grown near the city of Harrar in Ethiopia. (See "Coffees from Around the World," below.)

By contrast, terms such as *French, Viennese,* and *Italian* refer to the amount of roasting the beans received. Sound confusing? It is, and not just for consumers. Over the years, roasters have identified the different roasting stages with different names. Some use labels such as *French* and *Viennese,* because those countries have preferred that specific roast. Other roasters use names that describe the look and appearance of the roasted bean, such as *light, medium,* and *very dark* (see pages 24–25 for explanation of terms).

To add to the confusion, retailers also mix and name their own blends. These names usually have little to do with bean content and more to do with the seller's personal preferences. Alaska has yet to grow a coffee bean, but Yukon Blend is a popular Northwest coffee. If you find yourself floundering in a sea of roasts, blends, and beans, find a retailer who posts written descriptions or a salesperson who can explain the roasts so you can make an informed decision. Happy hunting!

coffees from around the world

The taste of a coffee bean, like that of a wine grape, depends on many factors, including climate, soil, altitude, growing conditions, and the human care given to the harvest. As with grapes, coffee beans have regional characteristics that the knowledgeable taster can identify. Here is a sampling of countries from the best-known coffee-growing regions.

brazil: It is the world's leading coffee producing country. Most beans are used in the production of canned and instant coffee. If you enjoy a mildly acidic, medium-bodied coffee, Bourbon Santos makes a fine brew.

colombia: Second to Brazil in worldwide production, Colombia is the largest exporter of hand-picked, washed arabica beans. Overall, these coffees have a clean, balanced flavor with medium acidity and make a good everyday choice.

costa rica: All of the beans from this Central American country are washed arabicas. Grown on the family-owned farms where many can export directly, the beans possess a rich, deep, full body and flavor.

guatemala: The mountainous volcanic soil of this Central American country nurture aromatic, mellow-bodied coffees. Grown in the regions of Antigua and Coban, the beans have a spicy flavor with hints of chocolate that many people feel makes the perfect cup of coffee.

hawaii: This is the only place in the United States with an ideal climate for growing coffee. The Kona district boasts the highest yield per tree in the world and produces an aromatic, subtle, mellow-bodied coffee.

ethiopia: According to legend, coffee's name came from the Ethiopian region of Kaffa. This country is Africa's major exporter of arabicas. These coffees are characterized by a floral aroma and a winy, lightly acidic, almost dry flavor that caresses your tongue like fine wine. Try a fragrant Ethiopian Harrar.

kenya: This African coffee, with its mellow, delicate smoothness, winy acidity and flavor overtones of berries, is popular in Europe as well as the United States.

yemen: This small country on the southern tip of the Aribian peninsula grows some of the world's most distinctive coffees. Mocha, named after the ancient Arabian port of Moka on the Red Sea, is distinctly fragrant and full-bodied. Shop carefully and be aware that genuine Mocha beans are rare.

java: One of the first world's coffee producers, this country's name is synonymous with the brew. World War II and disease decimated its famous arabica coffee crops, which were replaced with inferior robustas. Today, its arabicas produce earthy coffee with low acidity and smooth body.

sumatra: Earthy, rich and full-bodied, Sumatra's coffee is not timid. It can take, and often enjoys, the company of milk and sugar.

new guinea: Off the northern tip of Australia, this island began cultivating coffee in the 1930s with seeds from Jamaican Blue Mountain region. Its full body, moderate acidity, and well-rounded flavor makes it an excellent choice on its own or blended, especially for espresso.

the roast

Although tribesmen munched crushed coffee beans and animal fat as a trail staple, it was not until the thirteenth century that the secrets of roasting coffee were discovered. Unlike fragrant wine grapes or scented tea leaves, raw coffee beans conceal their flavor. Only with roasting are their flavors and aromas liberated.

Raw beans can be stored for years, but the roasted bean must be used quickly. So, up to the mid-nineteenth century, coffee drinkers and local shopkeepers roasted their beans over an open fire or in an oven in small batches. It was only after demand became concentrated in urban centers, where the distribution time was short, that large-scale roasting became practical.

The aroma of roasting coffee has not been without its dangers. In the late 1700s, Prussia's Frederick the Great banned the consumption of coffee by ordinary citizens. Forceful and prejudiced, he wanted his people to drink beer, the beverage of their fatherland, and he hired retired soldiers as coffee smellers to arrest anyone secretly roasting or brewing coffee. Frederick also encouraged physicians to report that coffee drinking caused sterility. This generated a famous musical protest, Bach's "Coffee Cantata." (Bach, a lover of coffee, was the father of twenty children.)

The principle of roasting coffee is quite simple: Heat raw beans between 380° and 480°F, when they begin to brown and their aromatic oils come to the surface. These water-soluble oils (also referred to as "solids") give coffee its flavor and aroma. Complexity and skill enter the equation because each variety of bean has its own ideal roasting time. While a roasting cylinder resembling a clothes dryer uniformly roasts the beans, the experienced roast master adjusts the temperature and roasting time according to sight, sound, and aroma.

After the beans have reached the desired roast, they are quickly dumped onto a perforated cooling table to avoid overcooking. A paddle keeps the beans revolving on the table, and a ventilator draws the hot air away. This is referred to as a dry roast. In contrast, large-scale commercial roasters frequently cool their beans with water jets. Naturally, this is referred to as a wet roast. Because the beans are hot, the water evaporates and cools the beans. However, if the water is sprayed after the beans have cooled too much, it can invade the beans, causing them to swell with unwanted moisture.

Although many commercial and specialty-coffee enterprises continue to roast their beans in small batches under the watchful eye and nose of a roast master, computerized roasting machines have crept into the larger market-place, cutting roasting times to one minute. Consequently, in the opinion of many coffee-lovers, the subtle nuances produced by the roast master are lost.

Some coffee-lovers can't resist the idea of roasting their own beans. I'm not one of them. I find the whole experience to be time-consuming and the results uneven. (Did I mention I also don't like pressing my own grapes to make wine?) But for those of you who do, there are a number of home roasting devices available, from stove-top models resembling old-fashioned

roasting stages

Light or *Cinnamon Roast* is the typical roast used for canned or institutional coffee, but it is also used for blends. In both cases, the beans have a dry, cinnamon-colored exterior.

Medium, City, Full-City, or *American Roast* is the all-purpose roast most Americans seem to prefer. The beans are medium brown in color, and their surface is dry. Although this brew may have snappy, acidic qualities, its flavor tends to be flat.

popcorn poppers to small electric roasters. If you are interested in learning more about home roasting, check out Sweet Maria's, a wonderfully detailed Web site (sweetmarias.com), or Corby Kummer's personal and informative section on home roasting in *The Joy of Coffee*; both are listed in Resources at the end of this book.

storing your beans

Your coffee beans' worst enemies are air and moisture. Once exposed to these vagrants, their flavorful oils vanish like New Year's resolutions. One way you can postpone their deterioration is to buy and store your beans whole. Another way to prevent flavor loss is to store loose beans in an opaque, airtight container that will hold them without leaving a large air space. You don't want to use the one-pound bag you bring home from the store. You do want to use a ceramic or plastic jar whose lid has a rubber gasket for an airtight closure.

Okay, I know there are those of you who don't or won't bother transferring your beans, because you're going to use them right away. Well, then, keep the ever-emptying bag snug around the beans with a rubber band, clothespin, or clip. And don't put the bag in the refrigerator.

Every time you move your coffee bean container in and out of the refrigerator, unwanted condensation may collect inside. That moisture will affect the bean's aromatic, water-soluble oils. If you refrigerate the beans in a permeable bag, you're also inviting any number of unwanted aromas to invade the bag and the beans. (When last night's pesto pasta shares shelf space with Major Dickason's Blend, your first-rate cup of French press may taste suspiciously of garlic.) Most coffee experts agree that if you will use

Full, High, Dark, Italian, Continental, or Viennese Roast is the favorite of many specialty-coffee stores because the taste strikes an even balance between sweetness and sharpness. The beans are chestnut brown in color and show patches of oil. Chicory is added to this roast to make a Louisiana-style coffee.

Espresso or *French Roast* is the darkest of all roasts. Its almost-black beans have a shiny, oily surface. All the acidic qualities and varietal coffee flavors are gone, but the pungent taste is a favorite of espresso-lovers.

your whole beans within 10 days, you should keep them in your kitchen or pantry in a cool, dry place, inside a snug, airtight container.

If you're tempted to buy more than an immediate supply of coffee, store the remainder in the freezer. Beans packaged in freezer bags will keep for several months. (But once you pull them out, keep them out.)

Since freshly roasted beans give off carbon dioxide, canned coffees are prestaled. In other words, the beans are allowed to sit out in the open so that the carbon dioxide dissipates. Unfortunately, so do the aromatic oils. No coffee-lover wants prestaled coffee, so most specialty-coffee roasters pack their whole and ground beans in a vacuum container with a one-way valve. This keeps the staling process at bay by releasing carbon dioxide without admitting moisture and oxygen.

The best way to tell if your beans are fresh is to use your nose. A sweet, earthy coffee aroma is what you want. If they have a dull, lifeless odor, put the beans back and find another store.

grinding your own

This takes so little time and the reward is so great. Grinding your own beans is the most significant thing you can do to improve the taste of your coffee. Typically, ground beans lose their vitality within one week. Grinding your own cuts down on the time their aromatic oils are exposed to the air: Before your beans lose their flavor, you will be delighting in a freshly brewed cup.

There are three basic types of home grinders: the mortar and pestle, the hand mill, and the electric grinder. For centuries, coffee drinkers used a mortar and pestle to grind their beans. Today it's considered time-consuming, and unless you are an expert, you'll produce an uneven grind. An old-fashioned alternative is a hand mill. Based on the same principle as a millstone, the hand mill was invented by the Turks in the fifteenth century to grind flour. You grind the beans by feeding them into the top of a box. A funnel or slotted screw drops the beans between two corrugated steel disks, one stationary, one rotated by a crank. As you turn the crank, the beans are crushed between the two disks and fall into a drawer at the bottom of the grinder. The fineness of the grind is determined by adjusting the spaces between the disks. Electric burr mills duplicate the action of the hand mill and give you a uniform grind at the touch of a button.

When you shop for an electric grinder, you'll find two types on the market: the burr style and the propeller style. The burr achieves a uniform grind, while the propeller grinder, which acts more like a mortar and pestle, creates granules of varying size. For this reason alone, many coffee-lovers will spend more on a burr grinder because they know that the best coffee — that is, the best extraction — is made from uniformly ground beans. A burr grinder costs about $60, while a propeller grinder sells for under $20. If cost is an issue, or if you already have the propeller style, grind your beans with on-off bursts (pretend it's a food processor) and gently shake the machine as it's grinding. This will help distribute the beans for uniform grinding as they are cut to smithereens.

The reason you grind coffee is to expose the beans' flavorful oils to hot water. Just how long the oils are in contact with the water depends on your brewing method. Every brewing method, whether infusion, espresso, or drip, exposes the beans for different periods of time. As a rule, the shorter the brewing time, the finer the grind.

One way to find out if your home grinder is giving you an accurate grind for your chosen brewing method is to compare it with a sample grind from a reputable coffee store. (Don't use an overworked, undermaintained supermarket grinder.) Look at and feel the difference. Rub the samples between your fingers. Do they feel the same? If there is a difference, adjust your grind accordingly. Here are some guidelines to help you decipher the difference between grinds.

Coarse: This grind's large granules are suited for a plunger (French press) or an open pot (cowboy coffee). The grind can range from the size of cracked black pepper to dry bread crumbs.

Medium: This grind resembles granulated sugar and is used primarily with a paper-filter drip, vacuum drip, or flip-drip pot (napoletana). It is the most versatile grind.

Fine/Espresso: With a texture between sand and table salt, this grind works well with stove-top espresso and electric-pump espresso makers.

Pulverized: Employed exclusively for Turkish coffee, this grind is as fine as flour. Most home grinders cannot crush beans this finely. Ask your coffee merchant to grind it for you, or buy a special Turkish grinder.

caffeine in coffee

If you find that your after-dinner demitasse keeps you awake or your office coffee gives you the jitters, caffeine may be the reason. Caffeine occurs naturally in many plants — coffee, tea, and cocoa, to name a few — and is a mildly habit-forming drug whose side effects have become a popular health issue in our culture. Controversial investigations have claimed that ingesting caffeine may lead to cancer, fibrocystic disease, heart attacks, and sterility, but there is no hard medical evidence that conclusively proves these allegations.

If you are trying to cut down on caffeine, but still want the pleasurable taste of coffee, there are some alternatives. The first may surprise you.

Robusta and arabica differ in the amount of caffeine they bring to a cup of coffee. Robusta, used primarily for canned and instant coffee, contains 2.5 percent caffeine; arabica contains only 1 percent. So, if your coffee comes in a can, dump it and replace it with less-stimulating arabica beans. The other alternative is to switch to decaf.

If you do decide to cut down on the amount of caffeine you drink, you may experience some withdrawal symptoms: a headache, drowsiness, even nausea. Don't worry; they're normal and will go away within a few days.

One-quarter of all the coffee drinkers in the United States drink decaffeinated coffee. During the past two decades, the techniques for removing caffeine from coffee beans have improved dramatically, giving us a rich, full-bodied brew. There are two basic ways of extracting caffeine: the direct method and the indirect method. Neither produces any measurable health risks.

In both instances, caffeine is brought to the surface of the green bean by treating it with warm water and steam; the caffeine is then eliminated by a water or solvent process. In the *indirect method,* the unroasted bean is soaked in a water solution, which removes caffeine along with other water-soluble components. In a separate step, this mixture is filtered through activated charcoal (the Swiss water process) or through a solvent, and the caffeine is segregated.

In the *direct method,* the softened bean is then treated with a solvent (methylene chloride), which binds with the caffeine before being rinsed or evaporated away. This is a faster, perhaps superior, method because it disturbs fewer of coffee's desirable components. However, one frequently raised concern is the possibility that residual chloride may be left on the roasted bean and consumed by the coffee drinker. You will be happy to know this is close to impossible, as the temperature for roasting coffee is 450°F, and methylene chloride evaporates at 170°F.

There are variations to each of these procedures, and if you're interested, your coffee merchant should be able to discuss the different methods. He or she will be one of the first to know of any significant changes in the decaffeinating process.

flavored coffee beans

To the purist, flavored gourmet coffees and wine coolers are kissing cousins. To new coffee drinkers, they're the entry-level beverage to the world of coffee. To the calorie-conscious, they're a treat without the calories. For best results, roasters add flavorings to freshly roasted beans while they are still warm and will absorb the additives easily. The flavors include chocolate, raspberry, vanilla, and mint — take your pick.

coffee additives

instant coffee

Instant coffee requires only a spoon, a cup, and some hot water. Other than convenience, it has little to recommend it. Most instant coffees are made from poor to mediocre beans brewed in industrial-sized percolators. The grounds are over-extracted, and much of the aroma and taste goes right up the smokestack. Aromatic oils must then be added back to the granules. The only real advantage to instant coffee is for use in recipes calling for coffee flavoring when no extra liquid is needed. Astronauts also find it handy.

An array of nuts, cereals, and vegetables have been tried at one time or another to extend or replace coffee. When coffee supplies became scarce during the Civil War, desperate Confederate soldiers used roasted sweet potato and Indian corn as a substitute. While the incentive for using a coffee substitute or extender is often cost, the motive for flavoring is to improve an inferior brew or to create a new taste. Two popular extenders that are also flavor enhancers are chicory and fig.

Chicory, the root of a plant related to our dandelion, is blended into some of the dark-roasted coffees of French, Cajun, and Vietnamese cuisines. Roasted chicory root has a peppery sharpness that gives even the darkest roasts a distinctive taste. Unlike the pungent aftertaste of chicory, roasted fig imparts a delicate fruity flavor to coffee. It is a popular blend in the United Kingdom, but is scarce in the United States.

the brew

There is nothing magical about brewing coffee. It's the same basic process, whether you plunk an inexpensive tin cup over a camp fire or switch on an elaborate espresso machine. You simply pour hot water over ground coffee long enough to extract the aromatic oils that will make the water taste good. All you really need, in addition to your beans, is a container for the water and, in most cases, a source of heat.

For over three hundred years, people have been inventing all kinds of gadgets to perform this simple task. The most popular — and a few of the most eccentric — brewing methods and tools are described later in this chapter. No matter which you choose, the following guidelines will help you to brew the best possible cup of coffee:

- Make sure your equipment is clean.
- Use fresh, cold water that tastes good.
- Use the correct grind and brewing time.
- Use the correct amount of coffee.
- Brew coffee at the correct water temperature.
- Serve the coffee right after making it.

Make Sure Your Equipment Is Clean. Remember the smell of the office coffee-pot you finally decided to clean? Or the first time you uncorked the picnic basket Thermos from last summer? Coffee contains oil. Every time you brew a pot, some of the residual oil is left in the container. If the oil in your coffeepot is not removed, it will affect every pot you brew, making it taste rancid and bitter.

So, rinse your pot thoroughly after each use with hot water and scrub it with a nonabrasive sponge, or use a little baking soda. Anytime you use an abrasive brush or cleaner, you scratch the interior surface of your pot. Those scratches trap unpleasant coffee oils and mineral deposits. (This is especially true with metal coffeepots. Porcelain and glass pots are less susceptible.) With daily use, you may want to wash your pot with soapy water every 7 to 10 days. If so, be sure to rinse it well with water. Soap or detergent can leave a film that will transform your Guatemalan Antigua into a perfumed impostor. After you've washed the pot, be sure to dry it. You might also want to rinse and dry the kettle to help prevent the buildup of mineral deposits.

Use Fresh, Cold, Water That Tastes Good. Coffee is 98 to 99 percent water. If the water flowing out of your kitchen faucet reminds you of a cool, crystal-clear mountain spring, it will make a great cup of coffee. When your water tastes bad, your coffee tastes worse.

If you use tap water, let it run a moment before filling your kettle. Although it is a much-argued point, I think warm tap water can have a slightly off taste from sediment in the hot-water tank, and so can cold water when it sits overnight in your water pipes. (It is also believed that warm water loses oxygen and becomes flat. That has not been my experience.) If you don't like the taste of your tap water, experiment with different bottled or filtered waters until you find one whose taste you enjoy. Brita makes a filtration pitcher, as well as a device that you can add to your faucet that removes chemicals like chlorine, which are bad for your health and have an off-flavor. The pitcher is inexpensive and widely available. By the way, don't use distilled water, the kind you use in a steam iron. It lacks minerals and tastes like air.

Use the Correct Grind and Brewing Time. To make a great cup of coffee, you have to extract the right amount of flavorful coffee oils or solids from the beans. They give coffee its flavor. Roasted beans contain about 30 percent solids; the ideal extract is between 18 and 22 percent. If this sounds like Chemistry 101, it isn't. You simply need to make sure that you use the correct grind and follow the correct brewing method to extract the flavor you want.

As you will learn in the following chapter, each brewing method — whether it's plunger, espresso, or drip — exposes the ground beans to hot water for different periods of time in order to achieve the correct extraction. Espresso is fast. Plunger is slow. Drip is in between. The faster the brewing time, the finer the grind needs to be. That's because a finer grind gives you more surface area, so the hot water moves easily and smoothly extracts the aromatic oils.

To determine the correct brewing time, get to know your brewing method. The easiest way is to read the instructions that come with your coffeepot or brewing machine. Another source is an informative coffee merchant or one of the many instructive Web sites devoted to the perfection of the brew (see "Resources," page 114).The most popular methods are described later in this chapter, along with their correct grind and brewing time.

Use the Correct Amount of Coffee. To make a full-flavored cup of coffee, use 2 level tablespoons of ground coffee (⅛ cup, or 1 Approved Coffee Measure) to 6 ounces of water. Keep in mind that 6 ounces will fill a normal cup but not a large mug. If you use a coffee scoop that you've purchased or that was included with your coffeemaker, be sure it measures 2 level tablespoons (some hold 1 tablespoon; others hold 3 to 4). If you like a weaker brew, make your coffee regular strength, then dilute with hot water. Don't use less coffee, because that will lead to over-extraction and a bitter cup. If you prefer stronger coffee, use more grounds.

Brew Coffee at the Correct Water Temperature. The reason you use hot, not boiling, water to brew your coffee is to draw out the beans' flavorful soluble oils. You don't want to cook the beans; that was done during the roasting process. The best brewing temperature for coffee is between 200° and 205°F, just below water's boiling point of 212°F. To reach that temperature, simply lift your kettle off the burner (or pull the plug) after it has reached a rapid boil, and hold it for 5 seconds before pouring the water over your grounds. If you use an automatic coffeemaker, remember that its thermostat has been set to brew with cold water.

Serve Coffee Right After Making It. The aroma and clean taste of that first cup you brew in the morning is a far cry from the mid-morning coffee you zap in the microwave. Within 15 minutes of brewing, the taste of coffee begins to deteriorate because the aromatic oils start to evaporate. After 40 minutes, you might as well give it the heave-ho. That's why I never use a burner to keep my coffee hot.

Preserving that first delicious brew is a challenge. One way is to use a water bath: Place a heat diffuser over very low heat, set a pan of hot water on top, and put the coffeepot inside the pan. The water bath works well for 15 minutes, enough time for a second cup. But the best way to keep your coffee hot for any length of time is in a preheated, vacuum-insulated thermal carafe. Many types and sizes are available, from fluted French flasks to sleek, stainless-steel Japanese canisters. If you are currently using an electric drip brewer and it's time to buy a new one, look for one that has a thermal carafe instead of a glass one. That way your coffee will stay fresher longer.

Finally, never reuse coffee grounds. It is like revisiting a past lover: Everything that was great has already been savored.

drip

The drip, or filter, method is one of the most popular ways to brew coffee. It is also one of the easiest. Whether you use an electric drip machine or do it manually, the principle is the same. The container has two parts. The filter is held in the upper section, or filter holder. You place ground coffee in the filter and pour hot water over the grounds. Gravity does the rest.

The Melitta paper filter system that dominates the market today was invented by a German housewife. In 1908, Melitta Bentz, after trying to filter the sediment out of her husband's coffee with a linen towel, substituted a sheet of blotter paper over a perforated brass bowl.

The kind of filter you use makes a big difference in the coffee you drink. Paper filters produce a clear, light-bodied brew because they trap the body-giving solids formed from the soluble oils. Paper filters also trap any sediment, and they make it easy to discard the grounds. They also assure a clean coffee-pot. The disadvantage to paper, besides having to periodically purchase the filters, is the flat, papery flavor that sometimes slips into your brew.

Your other choice is to use a metal filter. Think back to your last cup of espresso or French press. Remember the feel of the coffee in your mouth? That body comes from the solids. If you want that feel and taste from your drip coffee, invest in a metal filter. They come in different sizes and shapes (basket or cone), for either manual and electric models, and start at around $16 for a 23K gold-plated filter that will fit a 4-cup brewer. If you use an automatic drip machine, you may already be using a metal filter, since many incorporate them as standard equipment.

For my daily brew, I use a manual drip filter holder, a gold-mesh filter insert, and my handy Krups thermal carafe. I like my coffee a little strong, so I measure 2 scoops (¼ cup) medium-fine ground coffee (or medium ground, if I'm using a paper filter) for every 8 ounces of water. After preheating the carafe (by filling it with hot water and pouring the water out), I place the filter on the carafe. Next, I pour a small amount of water, just off the boil, over the grounds and let them settle for about 15 seconds. This helps to evenly wet the grounds and ensure maximum flavor. Then I add the remaining water, which drips through the filter. When the water has dripped through, I give the coffee a stir to distribute the heat and flavor throughout the pot, and get ready for a cup that really will be good to the last drop.

If you like the convenience of an automatic drip coffeemaker, there are a number of good ones on the market: Braun, Melitta, Krups, Mr. Coffee, and Salton, to name a few. If you are in the market for a new electric drip pot, it's important that you spend the money to buy a coffeemaker with at least 850 watts, and preferably 1,000. This is the only way to be assured that the heater is powerful enough to heat the water between 195° and 205°F. Otherwise, you'll end up with a weak, inferior brew. My only other word of advice is to look for a coffeemaker with a thermal carafe. Keeping your coffee hot on a burner is a sure-fire way to ruin it.

flip-drip

Get ready for some fun. Reminiscent of a childhood toy, the flip-drip pot makes a strong, rich cup of coffee. In the early nineteenth century, while most Europeans and Americans were steeping their coffee in an open pot, a French tinsmith invented the reversible drip coffeepot. The Italians were quick to adopt the clever contraption and named it the *napoletana macchinetta,* or Neapolitan flip-drip. The pot is composed of two metal cylinders and a filter basket compartment that fits snugly between them. One section, with the spout, pours. The other section acts as a boiler. Unfortunately, many of the pots are made of aluminum and if not cleaned properly will give off a metallic taste. So, if you decide to buy one, make sure it is made out of stainless steel.

When you make what has become Italy's household coffee, reverse it so that the spout section is on top. Fill the bottom section, or boiler, with cold water up to the tiny escape hole near the top. Insert the metal filter basket into the boiler and add medium-coarsely ground, Italian-roast coffee. For each 1½ cups water, the Italians use 3 scoops (6 tablespoons) ground coffee, which is why it tastes so strong. Once the basket is almost full and the coffee forms a mound, screw the filter basket cover on top of the coffee. Place the spout section over the filter compartment and snap it shut.

After the flip-drip has spent several minutes on medium heat, you will notice steam escaping from the hole on the side of the boiler. That's the signal that the water has reached the boil. Remove the pot from the heat, wait 20 seconds, then flip it over so that the top section with the spout is on the bottom. (Have some oven mitts handy in case the pot and its handles are too hot to touch.) In a few minutes, after the water has filtered through the ground coffee, give the brew a swirl and savor a great cup of coffee.

vacuum pot

This is quite possibly the most elegant way to brew good coffee. Suggesting a mode of life few of us have seen outside episodes of *Masterpiece Theatre,* the vacuum pot makes an unhurried ceremony of brewing coffee. An alchemist's dream, the vacuum pot was invented in 1840 by the Scottish marine scientist Robert Napier.

In the United States, an attractive stove-top vacuum brewer by Bodum, known as the Bodum Santos, is available in many specialty-coffee stores or on Web sites. (Starbucks also carries its version, the Barista Utopia, in its stores and online.) It comes with a stand and spirit lamp that make tabletop brewing possible. But the most elegant model, the British Cona, is the one to use. Made for a life of leisure, it works only by lamp. The 4-cup Cona retails for about $150 (see "Resources," page 116, under Sweet Maria's).

To experience this delectable pleasure yourself, take a hint from me. Instead of waiting for the water to boil using the spirit lamp (you'll be there all day), use your kettle. When the water has boiled, pour it into the lower pot. Use 2 tablespoons finely ground coffee for every 6 ounces of water. Add the ground coffee to the upper bowl, which has been fitted with a funnel and filter. Insert this precarious crucible into the lower pot, twist to create a seal, and place the pot over your heat source. When the water boils for the second time, rises in the funnel, and spills over the coffee grounds, stir the grounds and let the brew steep.

After 2 minutes, remove the pot from the heat source and watch the magic begin. The vacuum created in the lower pot draws the brewed coffee back through the filter and funnel. After several minutes, you will be ready to serve an exceptional cup of coffee that tastes both subtle and complex, as well as full-bodied.

plunger

The plunger pot, or French press, is my favorite way to make coffee when friends have joined my husband, Pete, and me for dinner or we're enjoying a leisurely breakfast. Besides looking splendid by candlelight or on a breakfast tray, this device makes a strong, full-bodied brew. That's because with a French press, the ground coffee beans are steeped in hot water, then strained through a metal filter that leaves just enough sediment to add body. In my mouth, it feels just this side of espresso. The plunger pot method employs the same principle used in brewing tea. It is also the method professional cuppers use to brew the coffee samples they're going to judge. With those kinds of recommendations, you know it's got to be good.

Since the pot cannot be placed directly on a heating element, and the grounds stay in contact with the water, the plunger pot is meant to brew coffee to enjoy immediately. So, it's important to buy the pot size that suits your needs. (There is even a 1-cup pot for the solo traveler.) To brew, preheat the plunger and pot with hot water. Measure 2 level tablespoons of fine- to medium-ground coffee per cup into the glass cylinder, or beaker. Pour 4 to 6 ounces of water just off the boil and stir the grounds with a wooden spoon to make sure all the grounds are wet. (A metal spoon can scratch or crack the beaker.) Then set the plunger on top of the beaker and allow the grounds to steep for 4 to 5 minutes.

Now, with a sure and steady hand, slowly press the plunger straight down. If you push at an angle, you can crack the beaker — I know, I speak from experience. If you have selected too fine a grind, pushing down the plunger can be an athletic feat. While you may find the workout well worth it, choose a coarser grind next time.

There are a few drawbacks to a plunger pot. It is a pain to clean. You have to unscrew and separate the filters and carefully wash the spent grounds from the beaker. Also, since the beaker is made out of glass and is not insulated (and the grounds stay in contact with the water), if you want hot coffee for longer than 10 minutes, you'll need to decant it into a thermal carafe.

While the plunger pot remains the most popular and sophisticated way to brew coffee by infusion, there are two other methods which are commonly used. They are the open pot, fondly known as cowboy or hobo coffee, and cold-water extraction.

open-pot, or cowboy coffee

The open-pot method is one of the oldest and simplest ways to brew coffee. All you need is water, ground coffee, heat, and a container. In many countries, this method remains the most widely used.

Originally, water was boiled vigorously with the grounds, but in the eighteenth century, the French discovered that steeping coffee made a much better brew. The only trick is separating the grounds before serving the coffee. Probably the easiest way is to use a strainer, but a clean sock will do, as will any number of other devices. In England, an egg white was dropped into the coffee, and the coagulating white seized most of the floating debris. In Scandinavian countries, fish skins were employed, along with their flavor. My suggestion is to pour a few tablespoons of cold water over the surface of your just-brewed coffee. The cold water falls, pulling most of the grounds to the bottom of your pot. Some buckaroos add a freshly broken eggshell with their coffee grounds to help clarify the brew.

To make cowboy coffee, combine 4 tablespoons coarsely ground coffee for each 2 cups of fresh water in a clean pot, and bring just to a boil. (Forget the legendary American West, where the unique aroma and taste came from a well-used, seldom-washed pot. Those residual coffee oils clinging to the coffeepot quickly turn bitter, and so does the coffee.) Give the grounds a stir to dissolve any lumps. Remove the container from the heat, cover, and let the coffee steep for 5 minutes. Strain, then serve in warmed mugs, preferably by a campfire.

cold-water extraction

This method produces a strong coffee concentrate. It is useful because you can store the concentrate in the refrigerator and make individual cups of coffee by diluting 2 tablespoons of concentrate with 8 ounces of water. The disadvantage to this method is that most of the aromatic oils brought out by hot water are not released in cold water, so this brew tends to taste bland and generic. To make cold-water concentrate, soak 1 pound ground coffee in 4 cups of cold water for 24 hours, then filter and refrigerate. To filter, use a large container and a filter cone, or buy a specially made brewer, such as the Toddy, which comes with a carafe, container, and two filters and sells for under $30.

ibrik or cezve

This brass or copper pot with its long, narrow handle is the traditional vessel used for making rich, strong Middle-Eastern coffee. You can make it in any pot, but there is a certain mystery and romance to the ritual of brewing in a Greek ibrik or Turkish cezve.

The method most commonly used today originated in the fifteenth century and is unique in several ways. First, spices such as cardamom, cinnamon, and nutmeg are often ground with the coffee beans to add exotic flavors, and sugar is added with the coffee grounds while brewing to make a sweet, syrupy drink. The coffee is next brought to a boil two or three times. In earlier days, Egyptian hosts would add a fragrant dollop of ambergris at the bottom of each cup, so the waxy substance would impart its perfume and its supposed powers as an aphrodisiac. Today, we stick to the more traditional method of brewing.

To brew, place 2 tablespoons pulverized, light-roasted coffee and 1 teaspoon to 1 tablespoon sugar in an ibrik or cezve. (If you don't have a Turkish grinder, buy coffee already pulverized from a shop.) Add 4 ounces of water and stir to dissolve the sugar. Make sure the ibrik is only half full, because as you gently boil your brew, foam will begin to rise and double.

After the coffee has come to a boil over low to medium heat, and the foam has reached the rim, about 2 minutes, remove the pot from the heat until the foam subsides, about 20 seconds. Repeat this once (Turkish style) or twice (Greek style), then allow the grounds to settle for 1 minute. Gently pour the coffee into 2-ounce demitasse cups so that some of the foam tops each cup. If you are careful, most of the grounds will stay in the pot.

percolator

A book on coffee isn't complete without the pumping percolator. Many Americans grew up with the familiar sound and fragrant smell of coffee brewing in a stove-top or electric percolator. Hardware and department stores still find shelf space for the pumping percolator, but you'll be hard-pressed to find one in any specialty-coffee store. At its pinnacle in the 1930s, the percolator's bubbling beat gave the impression of a happy home and a well-tended family. Little did we realize that those sounds and smells meant that the principles of brewing good coffee were unknown. The pumping percolator works by steam pressure, which continuously forces boiling water up a central tube and over the grounds. When this goes on for longer than 8 minutes, as it often does, the brew becomes bitter. Those fragrances wafting though the air are the aromas you should be enjoying in your cup.

At the 1855 Paris Exposition, the Edward Santais *caffè* espresso machine amazed visitors by making two thousand cups of coffee in one hour. While it may have been fast, the coffee was a big disappointment. The huge steam boilers forced hot water repeatedly through the coffee grounds, making the over-extracted drink bitter. It wasn't until 1946, when Achille Gaggia designed a machine with a mechanical source of pressure, the spring-powered piston, that it became possible to force hot (not boiling) water through coffee grounds quickly and powerfully enough to emulsify the beans' soluble oils and flavor components into a bittersweet brew that was velvety to the tongue.

The perfect cup of espresso requires beans, a machine, and a barista. The term *barista* is Italian, and in Italy, as in every other country where espresso is celebrated, the barista, or barperson, knows and understands the machine with a reverence equal to that of the cowboy's respect and affection for his horse. It's close to symbiosis. Baristas know that only with their constant care and maintenance, plus their intuitive judgment of their machine and the bean, are they able to create the perfect espresso and its crowning glory, *crema,* the caramel-colored foam that should lightly gild espresso.

Because making good espresso requires skill and expensive machinery, it is the coffee drink most often enjoyed outside the home. If you want to buy a home machine, there are a number of good choices (see "Resources," page 114). If you don't want to spend $200 to $400 or more but still want to make espresso-style coffee at home, consider the Moka (see page 50).

an espresso menu

Confused by coffeehouse menus or those drink orders you hear wait staff shouting to baristas? Here's a guide to let you know exactly what they mean.

- *Breve:* An espresso beverage made with half-and-half instead of milk.
- *Caffè:* In Italy, an espresso.
- *Caffè americano:* One or 2 shots of espresso with 6 ounces of hot water.
- *Caffè latte:* Half espresso, half hot milk, and no milk foam.
- *Caffè mocha:* One-third espresso, one-third hot chocolate, and one-third steamed milk.
- *Cappuccino:* One-third espresso, one-third steamed milk, and one-third milk foam.

- *Corretto:* Espresso "spiked" with grappa, brandy, or other liquor.
- *Doppio:* Two shots of espresso.
- *Cubano:* A doppio brewed with raw sugar.
- *Espresso:* Two tablespoons ground espresso with 1½ ounces water.
- *Espresso con panna:* Espresso topped with whipped cream.
- *Espresso romano:* Espresso served with a twist of lemon.
- *Macchiato:* Espresso "marked" with a spot or dollop of milk foam.
- *Latte macchiato:* Steamed milk "marked" with a spot of espresso.
- *Ristretto:* "Restricted," or extra-strength espresso: 2 tablespoons ground espresso with 2 ounces water.
- *Shakerato:* Espresso shaken with ice and sugar in a shaker.

Home espresso machines fall into two categories: the piston-style machine made by Pavoni and the pump-style espresso made by several manufacturers, including Faema, Bunn, Saeco, and Porteo. Let's start with the more sensible one, the pump-style. The real advantage to the pump is that it supplies the proper pressure so that anyone can make good espresso if he or she follows the manufacturer's directions. The biggest problem comes when the coffee is ground too coarsely, causing a watery brew. Pump machines also tend to be noisy, and like all home espresso machines, they are messy. You must constantly and meticulously keep cleaning them.

I use a piston-style Pavoni, and I freely admit that I'm attracted to its old-fashioned good looks and its specific ritual of making espresso. It reminds me of my father's pipe-smoking practices. Plus, there's an element of gambling, because the success of the espresso depends on the strength of my arm when I pull down the lever, and the lever is next to impossible to pull down if I've ground the beans too fine or I've packed them too tightly. Still, when I get it right, it's perfection.

To create the milk foam used in cappuccinos and lattes, commercial and home espresso machines have a device known as a steam wand. The wand brings steam from the boiler through a metal tube that is inserted into a container of cold milk. The barista opens the valve controlling the wand so that a steady stream of steam heats the milk and creates a fine, thick foam. Like making espresso, this takes skill. While following the manufacturer's directions is essential, producing exquisite milk foam has more to do with sight and sound, so experiment.

If you're thinking of investing in an espresso machine, do some homework, check the Web sites in the Resources section (page 114), and talk to coffee merchants you trust. Or, leave domestic mayhem behind, and wait in line for a barista to prepare the perfect cup for you.

moka

Not as highly fashioned as its festooned, copper-studded Italian relative, which inhabits noisy coffeehouses and chic bars, the simple, self-contained Moka stove-top pot makes a rich, aromatic brew in the unruffled atmosphere of your own kitchen. While the brew is not true espresso — it's more like double-strength coffee — the pot does use pressure to extract a body-giving texture and flavor that is close enough to satisfy millions of Italians who use it as their at-home *caffè* maker.

The Moka gets its pressure from boiling water in a closed chamber. The chamber, or base, has enough headroom to collect steam, and that steam creates enough pressure to force the hot water out of the base and through the grounds.

The Moka's smooth, heavy base works equally well on electric and gas stoves, and its inexpensive price (around $15 for a 6-demi-cup capacity) makes the delights of near-espresso available to everyone. Since you need to brew a full pot, buy the size that fits your needs. The original Moka pot is made of hard aluminum, which conducts heat efficiently but which some say can leave coffee with a metallic taste. Stainless-steel versions are available, but I confess that I still use the 2-cup aluminum version I bought years ago without noticing any adverse taste.

To make your *caffè*, unscrew the top of the Moka pot from its base, remove the filter funnel, and fill the base with fresh, cold water right up to the brass safety valve. Lightly pack and level off the funnel with medium-fine espresso roast and place the funnel back in the base. (The funnel is designed to take the correct measure. If it is not filled, you will end up with an unappealing, watery brown liquid.) Firmly screw the top onto the base and place the pot over medium-low heat.

As the water in the base begins to boil, in 3 to 5 minutes, pressure forces the water up through the grounds and the rich coffee begins to fill the upper chamber. When you hear a gurgling sound, you will know that all of the water has been forced up and out of the lower chamber and the coffee is ready to serve. You can check the progress of the water by opening the top and checking the flow of coffee. When the flow turns to foam, remove the pot from the heat. Once in a great while, if the stars are aligned and the gods are pleased, you may even find some *crema* floating on the surface of your cup.

recipes

advice to the cook

Coffee is the prime ingredient in dozens of delicious drinks and delectables, including cookies, cakes, breakfast pastries, candies, ice creams, and custards. Coffee is also the secret enhancer in certain savory foods, where its flavorful acids give life, strength, and sparkle to other ingredients.

Some ingredients have a natural affinity with coffee. Chocolate, for example, is a famous partner. Like a happy couple, chocolate and coffee bring out each other's best qualities. Other complementary companions include nuts such as hazelnuts, walnuts, and pecans, and citrus fruits such as oranges and lemons. When it comes to spices, the ones most widely used in coffee drinks and desserts are cardamom, ginger, and cinnamon. In savory dishes, you'll find that spices such as pepper, cumin, and paprika combine well with coffee.

Have you ever noticed that recipes using coffee as a flavoring, especially baked goods, call for instant coffee or instant espresso? Even coffee connoisseurs who shun the instant brew use it as a flavoring in their cakes and cookies. That's because the instant granules carry a concentrated punch that is difficult to obtain from a liquid beverage without adversely affecting the recipe.

When cooking with coffee, be sure to consider who is going to drink or eat it and when it's going to be served. You may want to use decaffeinated coffee if your recipe is served in the evening or if you're making it for children. The recipes in this chapter designate the type and strength to use. Refer to "Roasting Stages," pages 24 to 25, when a recipe requires a specific roast, and to "Coffee Grinds" on page 28 to 29 for specific grinds. The following list will help you to determine correct strengths.

Regular Strength	Two level tablespoons ground coffee or 2 teaspoons instant coffee to 6 ounces (¾ cup) water.
Extra Strength	Two level tablespoons ground coffee or 2 teaspoons instant coffee to 4 ounces (½ cup) water.
Double Strength	Four level tablespoons ground coffee or 4 teaspoons instant coffee to 6 ounces (¾ cup) water.
Espresso	Two level tablespoons ground espresso or 2 teaspoons instant espresso to 1½ ounces water.

right / toffee-coffee crunch brittle / see page 102

beverages

after-dinner drinks

café au lait

One of the pleasures of breakfast in France is a steaming bowl of café au lait. In Italy, it is called *caffè latte,* and it's made with 1 shot of espresso and scalded milk. In Spain, ask for *café con leche;* the milk will simply be heated.

for each drink, you will need :

1 cup 2-percent milk
1 cup hot, freshly brewed French-roast coffee

method :

In a small saucepan over medium heat, scald the milk. Pour the hot coffee and the hot milk simultaneously into a French café au lait bowl.

(If you like the milk blissfully frothy, you can purchase a pressurized steamer or frother.)

iced coffee

The secret to perfect iced coffee is to use cooled extra-strength coffee prepared no more than 3 hours in advance. If you use yesterday's surplus, you'll find it has lost its flavor and pizzazz.

For a variation, use coffee ice cubes: Freeze fresh leftover coffee into ice cubes and use them with regular-strength coffee. For a special treat, a scoop of vanilla ice cream gives a wonderful contrast in flavor and color — or try chocolate or coffee ice cream.

for each drink, you will need :

4 ice cubes
1 cup extra-strength brewed coffee,
    cooled to room temperature

method :

Put the ice cubes in a tall, chilled glass. Pour the coffee into the glass and serve.

thai kah-fe

In Thailand and Vietnam, coffee is a sweet, syrupy drink to enjoy after a deliciously spicy meal. In San Francisco, I had my first taste of *kah-fe,* which was made even sweeter when the restaurant owner added sugar syrup to the freshly brewed coffee.

In Thailand, coffee has a distinctive burnt flavor that comes from ground toasted sesame seeds and corn mixed with ground coffee. If you're interested in trying the authentic brew, look for Thai coffee powder in Asian markets.

for each drink, you will need :

⅓ cup sweetened condensed milk
   at room temperature
¾ cup hot double-strength French-roast
   brewed coffee

method :

Pour the condensed milk into a tall, preheated glass. Slowly pour the coffee so it slides down the inside of the glass. Stir the coffee and milk together or drink it black and white.

cappuccino borgia milkshake

serves 2 :

In the 1970s, Jim Roberts opened the first of many successful Oregon coffeehouses. He sold me my first espresso machine and showed me a multitude of ways to make great-tasting coffee drinks. This is one of Jim's originals and a favorite of mine. If you're not an espresso-lover, it also can be made with double-strength coffee.

¼ cup brewed espresso at room temperature

1½ cups chocolate ice cream

⅓ cup freshly squeezed orange juice

¼ cup whole milk

Lightly sweetened whipped cream, slivered or grated orange zest, and chocolate-covered espresso beans for garnish

method :

In a blender, combine the espresso, ice cream, orange juice, and milk. Blend just until smooth. Pour into 2 milkshake glasses and garnish each serving with whipped cream, orange zest, and a chocolate-covered espresso bean.

calypso smoothie

A banana has never had a more delicious or sophisticated persona than in this delectable drink. In the morning, omit the rum, substitute yogurt for the ice cream, and call it breakfast.

For each drink, you will need :

½ cup extra-strength brewed coffee
1 small ripe banana, sliced
1 large scoop (¾ cup) coffee or vanilla ice cream
2 tablespoons light or dark rum (optional)
Ground cinnamon for garnish

method :

Combine the coffee and banana in a blender and blend until smooth. Add the ice cream and rum, if desired. Blend at high speed until thick and smooth. Pour into a tall glass and sprinkle with cinnamon.

old-fashioned coffee soda

Here's a two-straw drink to share with your sweetheart.

For each drink, you will need :

1 cup chilled double-strength brewed coffee
1 teaspoon granulated or superfine sugar
⅓ cup half-and-half
1 large scoop (¾ cup) coffee ice cream
¼ to ⅓ cup chilled club soda
Sweetened whipped cream, shaved chocolate or chocolate sprinkles, and a maraschino cherry for garnish

method :

In a tall soda or malt glass, combine the coffee and sugar. Stir in the half-and-half. Add the ice cream and fill to the top with soda. Add a dollop of whipped cream, some shaved chocolate or sprinkles, and top with a cherry. Insert 2 straws.

turkish coffee float

With its combination of cola and coffee, this stimulating refreshment could be called a Caffeine Cooler. It might be the perfect solution to your next all-nighter. For those who don't wish to welcome the dawn, substitute the caffeine-free stuff. If you're wondering what kind of ice cream to use, I'd vote for peppermint candy or cinnamon swirl. (Okay, vanilla's good, too.)

For each drink, you will need :

½ cup chilled extra-strength brewed coffee

½ cup coffee or espresso ice cream (see page 101)

½ cup cola

Orange slice for garnish (optional)

method :

Pour the coffee into a glass. Add the ice cream, then the cola. Garnish with an orange slice, if you like. Insert a straw and have a spoon handy to sample the marvelous taste of melting ice cream swirling in coffee and cola.

I have always wanted to have one place where I could find any recipe I needed for an after-dinner coffee drink. So, here it is.

With the help of veteran bartender Matthew Meskel, some coffee-loving friends, and several comfy bar stools at Portland's Brasserie Montmartre, I spent many happy evenings collecting some wonderful coffee concoctions. It goes without saying that no two people mix a drink the same way, but Matthew and I have endeavored to give you formulas that will always taste good, plus some helpful tips for mixing classic after-dinner coffee drinks perfectly every time.

Tips for Perfect Coffee Cocktails

- For hot drinks, preheat the glassware with hot water.
- Use premium liquors and liqueurs.
- Use freshly brewed coffee or espresso.
- Use a calibrated jigger to accurately measure ingredients.
- Use unsweetened whipped cream in recipes calling for whipped cream. Unless it's specified in the recipe, sweetened whipped cream will compete with the flavors of the drink.

irish coffee

For each drink, you will need :

1 sugar cube

1½ to 2 ounces Irish whiskey

4 to 6 ounces hot coffee

Whipped cream for topping

method :

Put the sugar cube in the bottom of a coffee mug or a hot-drink glass. Pour the Irish whiskey over the cube. Fill with coffee and top with whipped cream.

Variation: A splash of Kahlúa can be substituted for the sugar cube.

jamaican coffee

For each drink, you will need :

¾ ounce Tía Maria

¾ ounce Myer's rum

4 to 6 ounces hot coffee

Whipped cream for topping

method :

Pour the Tía Maria and rum into a coffee mug or a hot-drink glass. Fill with coffee and top with whipped cream.

panamanian coffee

For each drink, you will need :

1 ounce Tía Maria

½ ounce crème de banane

4 to 6 ounces hot coffee

Whipped cream for topping

method :

Pour the Tía Maria and crème de banane into a
coffee mug or a hot-drink glass. Fill with coffee
and top with whipped cream.

mediterranean coffee

For each drink, you will need :

1 ounce Tuaca (Italian liqueur)

½ ounce amaretto

½ ounce Tía Maria

4 to 6 ounces hot coffee

Whipped cream for topping

method :

Pour the Tuaca, amaretto, and Tía Maria into a
coffee mug or a hot-drink glass. Fill with coffee
and top with whipped cream.

international coffee

For each drink, you will need :

½ ounce Metaxa (sweet Greek brandy)

½ ounce Cointreau

½ ounce Tía Maria

4 to 6 ounces hot coffee

Whipped cream for topping

method :

Pour the Metaxa, Cointreau, and Tía Maria into a coffee mug or a hot-drink glass. Fill with coffee and top with whipped cream.

kioki coffee

For each drink, you will need :

½ ounce brandy

¾ ounce Kahlúa

4 to 6 ounces hot coffee

Whipped cream for topping

method :

Pour the brandy and Kahlúa into a coffee mug or a hot drink glass. Fill with coffee and top with whipped cream.

coffee nudge

¾ ounce Kahlúa

½ ounce dark crème de cacao

¼ ounce brandy

4 to 6 ounces hot coffee

Whipped cream for topping

method :

Pour the Kahlúa, crème de cacao, and brandy into a coffee mug or a hot-drink glass. Fill with coffee and top with whipped cream.

french nudge

For each drink, you will need :

½ ounce Kahlúa

½ ounce dark crème de cacao

¼ ounce Grand Marnier

4 to 6 ounces hot coffee

Whipped cream for topping

method :

Pour the Kahlúa, crème de cacao, and Grand Marnier into a coffee mug or a hot-drink glass. Fill with coffee and top with whipped cream.

a nutty irishman

For each drink, you will need :

¾ ounce Bailey's Original Irish Cream

¾ ounce Frangelico

4 to 6 ounces hot coffee

Whipped cream for topping

method :

Pour the Irish Cream and Frangelico into a coffee mug or a hot-drink glass. Fill with coffee and top with whipped cream.

b-52 coffee

For each drink, you will need :

½ ounce Kahlúa

½ ounce Bailey's Original Irish Cream

½ ounce Grand Marnier

4 to 6 ounces hot coffee

Whipped cream for topping

method :

Pour the Kahlúa, Irish Cream, and Grand Marnier into a coffee mug or a hot-drink glass. Fill with coffee and top with whipped cream.

coffee cloud

For each drink, you will need :

¾ ounce Kahlúa

¾ ounce Bailey's Original Irish Cream

4 to 6 ounces hot coffee

Whipped cream for topping

method :

Pour the Kahlúa and Irish Cream into a coffee mug or a hot-drink glass. Fill with coffee and top with whipped cream.

mexican coffee

For each drink, you will need :

¾ ounce Kahlúa

¾ ounce Cuervo Gold tequila

4 to 6 ounces hot coffee

Whipped cream for topping

method :

Pour the Kahlúa and tequila into a coffee mug or a hot-drink glass. Fill with coffee and top with whipped cream.

drunken padre

For each drink, you will need :

½ ounce Cuervo Gold tequila

½ ounce Frangelico liqueur

½ ounce Bailey's Original Irish Cream

4 to 6 ounces hot coffee

Whipped cream for topping

method :

Pour the tequila, Frangelico, and Irish Cream into a coffee mug or a hot-drink glass. Fill with coffee and top with whipped cream.

espresso martini

The bar was closing. "Come on, let's have some fun," someone said. "Let's think up an espresso martini." It sounded good to us, but we wondered what to use for an olive.

For each drink, you will need :

ice cubes

1 ounce vodka

½ ounce Kahlúa

1 ounce hot espresso

lightly whipped cream for topping

1 malted milk ball (do you have a better idea?), optional

method :

Fill a mixing glass or shaker with ice. Add the vodka, Kahlúa, and espresso. Shake, then strain into a chilled martini glass. Top with a layer of whipped cream and garnish with the malted milk ball, if desired.

kaffe cardamom

This after-dinner drink delivers a sweet, aromatic hint of cardamom. Reminiscent of ginger but less peppery, cardamom is a popular spice used in many cuisines, including Scandinavian, Arabic, and East Indian. Besides its appealing aroma, cardamom aids digestion and the tiny seeds, when chewed, sweeten your breath. Next time you dine at an East Indian restaurant, you may notice a small bowl of cardamom pods at the counter. They are there to be enjoyed by customers, much like after-dinner mints.

serves 4 :

seeds from 4 cardamom pods

¼ cup Cognac

2 tablespoons curaçao

1 tablespoon sugar

2 cups hot extra-strength coffee

method :

In a small saucepan, combine the cardamom seeds, Cognac, curaçao, and sugar. Heat over low heat until hot. Remove from heat. With a long-handled match, set the liquid aflame and let burn for 10 seconds. Add the coffee to the mixture and stir. Pour into demitasse cups and savor the bouquet and taste.

desserts

good-morning orange cake

Here's a delicious way to start your day, especially when you take time to brew a rich, fragrant cup of French-press coffee. An orange-scented aroma will fill your kitchen whenever you bake this simple Italian breakfast cake.

The olive oil makes this cake extra moist. "Olive oil in a cake?" you say. Olive oil is the heart, soul, and foundation of Italian cooking. You can find it in virtually every dish, from dipping sauce to pasta, meat, and seafood. Desserts and baked goods are made with it because its aromatic flavor enlivens and accentuates the other ingredients.

1 cup all-purpose flour

¼ teaspoon baking powder

¼ teaspoon baking soda

Pinch of salt

2 eggs at room temperature

1 cup granulated sugar

½ cup extra-virgin Italian olive oil

¾ cup milk

Grated or shredded zest of 3 oranges

Garnish:

Powdered sugar for dusting

Shredded zest of 1 orange

2 oranges, peeled and cut into ¼-inch-thick
   crosswise slices

(continued)

Preheat the oven to 350°F. Lightly grease the
bottom and sides of a 9-inch round cake pan. Line
the bottom with a round of parchment or waxed
paper. Grease the paper and set aside.

In a large bowl, whisk the flour, baking
powder, baking soda, and salt together. Set aside.

In a medium bowl, whisk the eggs and
granulated sugar together until blended. Whisk
in the olive oil, milk, and orange zest. Stir the
egg mixture into the flour mixture and mix until
just blended. Pour the batter into the prepared
pan and bake until the cake is firm and a toothpick inserted into the center comes out clean,
about 30 minutes. Transfer the pan to a wire rack
and let the cake cool for 10 minutes.

To serve, unmold the cake, remove the
parchment paper, and place the cake on a serving
plate. Sift powdered sugar evenly over the top,
letting some fall onto the plate. Garnish the top
of the cake with a sprinkling of orange zest and
surround it with the orange slices.

chocolate-cinnamon biscotti

We Americans have trouble resisting coffee and chocolate. Thanks to the Italians and their famous dunking cookies, we can have both. The nutty sweetness of almonds and a touch of cinnamon make these dunking cookies superb any time of day. If you like your biscotti slightly chewy, bake them only once. They're terrific either way.

1¼ cups all-purpose flour

¾ cup sugar, plus 1 teaspoon for garnish

¼ cup unsweetened cocoa powder

1 tablespoon ground cinnamon

¾ teaspoon baking powder

Pinch of salt

4 tablespoons unsalted butter at room
   temperature

3 egg whites

1 to 2 teaspoons water, if needed

¼ cup slivered almonds, toasted (see page 81)

method :

Preheat the oven to 350°F. Line a baking sheet with parchment paper or grease it.

In a bowl, whisk the flour, sugar, cocoa, cinnamon, baking powder, and salt together. Using a hand-held electric mixer on medium speed or your fingers, work the butter into the flour mixture until crumbly. Beat in 2 of the egg whites until a soft dough forms, about 1 minute. (If the dough doesn't stick together, stir in 1 to 2 teaspoons water.) Stir in the almonds.

With lightly floured hands, gather the dough and place it on a lightly floured surface. Shape the dough into two 9-inch logs. Place on the prepared baking sheet and flatten slightly to a 2-inch width.

In a cup or small bowl, lightly beat the remaining egg white until foamy and brush it over the logs. Sprinkle with the 1 teaspoon sugar. Bake the logs until firm, 30 to 35 minutes. Slide each log onto a wire rack to cool for 8 to 10 minutes.

(If you like your biscotti slightly chewy, disregard the next baking.)

Reduce the oven temperature to 325°F. Transfer a log to a cutting board. Using a serrated knife, slice into ½-inch-thick diagonal pieces. Place, cut-side down, on the baking sheet, and bake until crisp, about 15 minutes. Transfer from baking sheet to a wire rack to cool completely. Repeat with the remaining log. Store in a tightly covered container.

little wing's quaresimali

I first tasted these crisp, nut-studded biscotti at the Little Wing's Cafe in Portland, Oregon, and the owners, Bob and Barbara Weisman, graciously shared their recipe. It includes a little butter, which makes the name a bit of a misnomer: These Italian cookies were originally made without butter and were intended as a token of abstinence during Lent (*quaresima*). You can enjoy them as an indulgence instead. Note that the cookies are baked once, not twice, like traditional biscotti.

2 cups cake flour

2 cups sugar

1 teaspoon baking powder

1 teaspoon ground cardamom

2½ tablespoons unsalted butter at room temperature

2 cups sliced almonds, toasted (recipe follows)

2 cups hazelnuts, toasted and skinned (recipe follows)

3 eggs at room temperature, lightly beaten

1 teaspoon almond extract

method :

Preheat the oven to 350°F. Line 2 baking sheets with parchment paper or grease them.

In a bowl, whisk the flour, sugar, baking powder, and cardamom together. Using a pastry blender, 2 knives, or your fingertips, cut or blend in the butter until the mixture is crumbly. Stir in the almonds and hazelnuts. In a small bowl, whisk the eggs and almond extract together. Stir the egg mixture into the flour mixture to make a moist, sticky dough.

Scoop one-third of the sticky dough out onto a lightly floured surface. Lightly flour your hands and shape the dough into two 9-inch-long logs. Place the 2 logs on the prepared pan, 3 inches apart and at least 2 inches from the edge because they will spread during baking. Flatten each log to a 2½-inch width. Scoop out another third of the dough and repeat, using the second baking sheet. (Repeat with the last third of the dough after the first baking sheet is free.)

Bake the logs until they are light brown and the middle is not too soft, 25 to 30 minutes.

Don't worry if they touch. Let cool for 8 to 10 minutes. If the logs are touching, cut them apart with a knife. Carefully transfer to a cutting board. Using a serrated knife, cut each log into ½-inch-thick diagonal slices. Transfer to a wire rack to cool completely. Store in an airtight container.

For crisper cookies, reduce the oven temperature to 325°F. Place the cookies, cut-side down, on the baking sheet and bake until crisp, about 15 minutes.

toasting almonds: Preheat the oven to 350°F. Spread the nuts on a rimmed baking sheet and bake until lightly browned, 8 to 10 minutes.

toasting and skinning hazelnuts: Preheat the oven to 350°F. Spread the nuts on a rimmed baking sheet and bake until the skins crack and the nuts brown, 10 to 15 minutes. Wrap the nuts in a kitchen towel and let "steam" for 5 minutes. Rub the towel firmly between your hands, which will cause most of the skins to flake off.

snow-cap cookies

In some circles, these rich, chewy cookies are known as chocolate crinkles because each cookie acquires a crinkled white topping during the baking process. In this recipe, dark chocolate and espresso make the contrast even greater, giving the cookies a snow-capped appearance and a superb flavor. If you're a real chocolate-lover, try adding semisweet chocolate chips to the dough before chilling. You won't be sorry.

makes about 2½ dozen cookies :

4 tablespoons unsalted butter

2 ounces unsweetened chocolate, chopped

2 eggs at room temperature

1 teaspoon vanilla extract

1 tablespoon instant espresso powder

1 cup granulated sugar

1 cup all-purpose flour

1 teaspoon baking powder

¼ teaspoon salt

½ cup sifted powdered sugar

method :

In a small saucepan melt the butter and chocolate over low heat. Stir to blend and set aside to cool slightly.

In a medium bowl combine the eggs, vanilla, espresso powder, and granulated sugar. Using an electric mixer on medium speed, beat until light and fluffy, about 3 minutes. In another bowl, whisk together the flour, baking powder, and salt. Alternately blend the dry ingredients and the chocolate mixture into the egg mixture in three increments. Cover and refrigerate until firm, at least 3 hours.

Preheat the oven to 350°F. Shape the chilled dough into 1-inch balls and roll in the powdered sugar to form a thick coat. Place about 2 inches apart on an ungreased baking sheet. Bake until set, about 15 minutes. Transfer to a wire rack and let cool completely.

candied ginger shortbread

Ginger has been pleasing palates since the ancient Greeks first made gingerbread. In this recipe, crystallized ginger and ground ginger give buttery shortbread a peppery and slightly sweet taste. The cold butter is grated into the flour mixture. The result is a flakier cookie; it's much easier to incorporate into the dry ingredients, and it remains cold.

1¼ cups all-purpose flour

¼ cup plus 1 to 2 teaspoons superfine sugar
   (or granulated sugar processed for 10 seconds
   in a blender or mini-food processor)

3 tablespoons cornstarch

2½ teaspoons ground ginger

Pinch of salt

2 tablespoons coarsely chopped crystallized ginger

½ cup (1 stick) plus 2 tablespoons frozen
   unsalted butter

(continued)

Preheat the oven to 325°F. Set aside a 9-inch round cake pan with a removable bottom or line a 9-inch round cake pan with a round of parchment paper.

In a medium bowl, whisk the flour, the ¼ cup sugar, the cornstarch, ground ginger, and salt together. Stir in the crystallized ginger. Using the large holes of a flat or four-sided grater, grate the butter into the flour mixture. With your fingertips, work the mixture together until it is crumbly and the butter begins to soften. Continue to work until the dough can be packed into a ball.

Put the mixture into the prepared pan. Press to an even thickness, covering the bottom of the pan. Pierce the dough all over with a fork. Bake until golden, about 35 minutes. Immediately sprinkle 1 to 2 teaspoons sugar over the surface. Use a sharp knife to cut into 12 wedges. Let cool in the pan for 15 minutes. Unmold and transfer to a wire rack to cool completely. Store in an airtight container.

bittersweet chocolate-ginger shortbread: Prepare the above cookies and let cool. Melt 2 ounces chopped bittersweet chocolate in a double boiler over barely simmering water. Dust the crumbs off each cookie with a pastry brush and dip the outer edge of each cookie into the melted chocolate. Sprinkle with additional chopped crystallized ginger and place on a wire rack until the chocolate has set.

gelato affogato

This dessert ignited an irresistible craving. Oregon pastry chef Mandy Groom first made me *gelato affogato* at Zefiro's Restaurant in Portland. She used Illy espresso and her homemade vanilla-bean ice cream. Amazing. The next time I ordered dessert, I skipped over the creamy brulées, decadent cakes, and fresh fruit sorbets, and headed right for her *affogato di giorno*. She made it with cinnamon ice cream, or was it caramel? Either way, I was hooked.

If you have an espresso machine, this is one of the simplest (and best) coffee desserts you can make. It's served in a glass, and you use a spoon to dip down and taste each layer, then hold the glass like a beverage and sip. Cool, creamy, hot, rich, deep, dark, and delicious: They're all here in one fantastic dessert.

to make each dessert, you will need :

2 scoops ice cream of your choice, such as
   vanilla, cinnamon, caramel, or espresso
   (page 101)
2 shots hot espresso
⅓ cup lightly sweetened softly whipped cream
2 chocolate-coated espresso beans for garnish

method :

Put the ice cream in an old-fashioned glass. Pour the hot espresso over the ice cream. Top with the whipped cream and garnish with the espresso beans.

panna cotta al caffè

Smooth and silky, easy and elegant, the jellied confection known as *panna cotta* is the quintessential Italian dessert. In Italy, the classic flavors are almond and vanilla. In this recipe, espresso and Kahlúa give the dessert a sophisticated taste that's somewhere between a delightful after-dinner drink and a marvelous mocha mousse.

1 package (2 teaspoons) unflavored gelatin

1 cup milk or half-and-half

1½ cups heavy (whipping) cream

¼ cup sugar

1 tablespoon plus 2 teaspoons instant
    espresso powder

3 tablespoons Kahlúa or Tía Maria liqueur

Optional Garnishes:

Sweetened whipped cream

6 chocolate-covered espresso beans or
    lemon twists

method :

Set aside six ½-cup ramekins or stemmed wine glasses. In a small bowl or glass measuring cup, sprinkle the gelatin over the milk or half-and-half. Let stand until the gelatin softens and absorbs the liquid, about 5 minutes. Lightly stir to break up the gelatin.

In a medium saucepan, combine the cream, sugar, and espresso powder. Cook over medium-low heat, stirring occasionally, until the mixture just reaches a boil. Remove from heat. Whisk in the gelatin mixture until the gelatin is completely dissolved. If necessary, briefly reheat the mixture over low heat to dissolve the gelatin. Stir in the Kahlúa or Tía Maria. Pour the mixture into a pitcher and let cool to room temperature. Stir to blend. Fill the ramekins or glasses. Refrigerate for at least 4 hours or until set, or as long as overnight.

Serve as is, or top with a dollop of whipped cream and a chocolate-covered espresso bean or lemon twist.

cappuccino custard sauce

This heavenly custard is my favorite dessert sauce. I'll think of any excuse to make it. The rich yet not-too-sweet flavor complements many desserts, and the sauce is divine drizzled over angel food cake, crepes, or simple meringues.

makes about 1¾ cups :

1½ cups heavy (whipping) cream

1 tablespoon plus 2 teaspoons instant
   espresso powder

4 egg yolks

¼ cup sugar

1 tablespoon Grand Marnier or to taste

method :

In a double boiler over simmering water, heat the cream and espresso powder until small bubbles appear around the edges of the pan.

Meanwhile, in a medium bowl, beat the egg yolks and sugar until smooth and blended, 1½ to 2 minutes. Gradually drizzle ½ cup of the hot cream into the yolk mixture, stirring constantly. Gradually whisk the yolk mixture into the hot cream in the pan. Cook over simmering water, stirring constantly, until the custard thickens, about 10 minutes. To check for doneness, draw your finger through the custard on the back of the spoon; it should leave a trail.

Strain the custard through a fine-meshed sieve. Stir in the Grand Marnier. Serve warm or chilled. To store, cover and refrigerate for up to 3 days.

silverton chocolate cake

Virtually all the hazelnuts grown in North America come from fertile valleys in Oregon, like the ones near the town of Silverton. Hazelnuts, also known as filberts, have a rich flavor that complements the bittersweet flavors of semisweet chocolate and espresso. This delicately textured, moist cake is best the day after baking, when all the flavors have had a chance to mellow.

¾ cup freshly brewed espresso or

    2 tablespoons instant coffee powder

    dissolved in ¾ cup boiling water

4 ounces semisweet chocolate, chopped

2 tablespoons instant coffee powder

6 tablespoons unsalted butter

3 eggs, separated and at room temperature

½ cup granulated sugar

¾ cup plus 2 tablespoons hazelnuts, toasted

    and peeled (see page 81)

6 tablespoons all-purpose flour

2 tablespoons unsweetened cocoa powder

1 egg white

Pinch of salt

Powdered sugar for dusting

method :

Preheat the oven to 350°F. Lightly grease the bottom and sides of a 9-inch round cake pan. Line the bottom with a round of parchment or waxed paper. Grease the paper and set aside.

In a saucepan over low heat, combine the brewed espresso, chocolate, coffee powder, and butter, stirring occasionally, until melted. Set aside to cool.

In a medium bowl, whisk the egg yolks and granulated sugar together until pale and fluffy. Slowly whisk the chocolate mixture into the egg mixture until blended.

In a food processor, process the ¾ cup nuts until finely chopped, about 20 seconds. Add the flour and cocoa, and process for 10 more seconds. Measure out 1 cup of the chocolate batter. With the machine running, gradually add the mixture to the food processor through the feed tube to form a paste. Stir the paste back into the batter and beat until well blended.

In a large bowl, beat the 4 egg whites with the salt until stiff, glossy peaks form. Whisk about one-quarter of the beaten whites into the batter. Using a rubber spatula, fold in the remaining whites until blended. Pour the batter into the prepared pan and bake until firm, about 30 minutes. A toothpick inserted in the center should come out slightly sticky. Transfer the pan to a wire rack and let the cake cool. Unmold, remove the parchment paper, and place the cake on a plate. Chop the remaining 2 tablespoons nuts and sprinkle on the cake along with the powdered sugar.

granita di caffé

When the summer sun is blazing, there's nothing better than the refreshing taste of frozen espresso crystals melting in your mouth. In Italy, this dessert is known as granita. The Italians relax after lunch at an outdoor cafe with a glass of granita and a tiny spoon, enjoying each other's company and life's daily parade. Wouldn't we all like to follow that routine?

serves 2 to 4 :

¼ cup plus 2 tablespoons (2 shots) freshly brewed espresso

⅔ cup hot water

2 tablespoons sugar or more to taste

method :

Combine the espresso, water, and sugar. Stir to dissolve the sugar and taste. The flavor should be semisweet. Let cool to room temperature.

Pour the espresso mixture into a 9-by-5-inch loaf pan and place it in the freezer. After 30 minutes, remove the pan from the freezer and stir to break up the ice crystals. Return to the freezer and repeat every 30 minutes over a period of 1½ to 2 hours, until the ice acquires a firm, smooth consistency. (This isn't as tedious as it sounds. In fact, it's interesting to see how the ice crystals form and turn almost fluffy.)

To serve, scoop into glasses or demitasse cups. For best results, serve the granita the same day you make it.

Granita di limone: Using this same technique, you can make another one of Italy's favorite refreshments: Combine 1½ cups water, ½ cup fresh lemon juice, and 5 tablespoons sugar. Proceed as in the above recipe.

devil's halos

Here is a sinfully rich dessert that's as marvelous to look at as it is to eat. Its name refers to the devilishly good, halo-shaped mocha meringues, which hold a scoop of rich ice cream and hot fudge sauce. Leap into Lucifer's lair and let your taste buds luxuriate. If you like, substitute coffee or vanilla ice cream for the espresso ice cream.

Meringue Halos:

¾ cup sugar

2 to 3 tablespoons unsweetenend Dutch-process
   cocoa powder

1½ teaspoons instant coffee powder

3 egg whites

⅜ teaspoon cream of tartar

Molten Fudge Sauce:

6 ounces bittersweet chocolate, preferably
   Scharffen Berger or Lindt, chopped

¼ cup plus 2 tablespoons double-strength
   brewed coffee

2 tablespoons sugar

Espresso Ice Cream (page 101)

Optional Garnishes:

Lightly sweetened whipped cream

Toasted almonds, toasted pecans, or
   Toffee-Coffee Crunch Brittle (page 102),
   crushed

(continued)

method :

To make the halos: Preheat the oven to 200°F. Line a baking sheet with parchment paper. Draw six 3½-inch circles on the paper, leaving at least 1 inch between them.

In a small bowl, whisk the sugar, cocoa, and coffee powder together and set aside. In the bowl of a standing mixer fitted with a whisk, on medium-low speed, beat the egg whites and cream of tartar until frothy, about 1½ minutes. Increase the speed to medium-high, and slowly add the sugar mixture, whisking until stiff, about 2½ minutes. Increase the speed to high, and continue to whisk until stiff and glossy, about 4 minutes.

For each halo, use a teaspoon to drop a 1-inch dollop of meringue onto the outlined circle. Drop a second spoonful next to the first so that they connect. Repeat to form a circle, using about 10 dollops per circle. Repeat to form other circles. Make individual meringue kisses with the leftover meringue. Bake for 2½ to 3 hours, or until dry throughout. Test by checking one of the kisses. If the halos need to dry further, turn off the oven and leave them inside, with the door shut, for 30 to 90 minutes. Transfer to wire racks to cool completely. Store in an airtight container for up to 2 weeks.

To make the fudge sauce: In a small, heavy saucepan melt the chocolate and coffee over low heat, stirring until smooth. Add the sugar and stir until blended and dissolved. Remove from heat and let cool to warm.

To assemble, place each meringue halo on a dessert plate. Place a scoop of ice cream in the center of each halo. Drizzle the warm sauce over the ice cream. Garnish with whipped cream and a sprinkling of crushed nuts or candy, if you like.

devil's kisses: For a delicious, low-fat cookie, follow the above recipe but instead of forming halos, make 2½-inch individual kisses. Makes about 30 kisses.

kiss and tell: Dip cooled Devil's Kisses, above, in melted bittersweet chocolate and dust with a pinch of finely ground coffee.

sweet-and-easy
cinnamon twists

It's morning. The coffee's freshly ground and ready to brew, and all you want is a taste or two of something sweet. These cinnamon pastries are the ideal answer. With a little help from the freezer section of your supermarket, they go together in minutes. So, twist up a batch for yourself, for family, for friends at the office.

makes 6 twists :

1 sheet thawed frozen puff pastry, 9½ by
   10 inches (see note)
1 egg, lightly beaten
4 tablespoons sugar mixed with 2 teaspoons
   ground cinnamon

method :

Preheat the oven to 400°F. Line a baking sheet with parchment paper or grease it.

On a floured surface, unfold the pastry sheet and roll it out into a 10-by-14-inch rectangle. Cut in half lengthwise. Brush both halves with the egg. Top one half with 3 tablespoons of the sugar mixture. Place the remaining pastry half, coated-side down, over the filling. To seal, gently roll with a rolling pin.

Cut six 1-inch lengthwise strips of pastry. Twist a strip 4 to 6 times for a wide, loose twist, or 10 to 12 times for a breadstick-style twist. Place it on the prepared baking sheet, pressing the ends down. Repeat with remaining strips, leaving 2 inches between strips. Brush the strips with more egg and sprinkle the remaining sugar mixture over them. Bake until golden brown, about 15 minutes. Let the twists cool for 10 minutes to let the centers crisp. Serve warm or at room temperature.

Note: Frozen puff pastry can be found in the freezer section of most supermarkets. Pepperidge Farm's 17.3-ounce package contains 2 sheets.

tiramisù

Look no farther for the perfect tiramisù. You've just found it. Whenever I spot the rich layered Italian dessert on a restaurant menu, I always order it, but I've never found one to equal this version, given to me by Joann Vazquez, the head pastry chef at Marsee Baking Company in Portland, Oregon. Vazquez's recipe for the Tuscan trifle is a grown-up's delight with its combination of mascarpone cream, coffee-rum-soaked lady fingers, and the chilled wine custard known as zabaglione.

Zabaglione:

4 egg yolks

¼ cup granulated sugar

¼ cup sweet Marsala

Mascarpone Cream:

1 cup (8 ounces) mascarpone cheese
    at room temperature

1¼ cups heavy (whipping) cream

6 tablespoons powdered sugar

½ teaspoon vanilla extract

½ cup freshly brewed espresso, or
    1½ tablespoons instant coffee powder
    dissolved in ½ cup boiling water

1 tablespoon granulated sugar

½ cup light or dark rum

16 to 20 ladyfingers

Unsweetened cocoa powder for dusting

(continued)

To make the zabaglione: In a double boiler, combine the egg yolks with the granulated sugar. Beat with a whisk until pale, about 3 minutes. Place over barely simmering water and add the Marsala, whisking continuously until the mixture is thick, foamy, and warm to the touch. Remove from heat and continue whisking until the zabaglione has cooled slightly. Set aside.

To make the mascarpone cream: In a small bowl, beat the cheese until smooth and set aside. In a large bowl, beat the cream until soft peaks form. Blend in the cheese, powdered sugar, and vanilla. Beat until well blended and stiff. Set aside.

In a small bowl, combine the espresso, granulated sugar, and rum. Set aside.

To assemble, line the bottom of an 8-cup bowl or oblong pan with one-third of the ladyfingers, laying them flat. Drizzle one-third of the espresso mixture evenly over the ladyfingers and let set for several minutes. Spread one-third of the mascarpone cream evenly over the ladyfingers, then spread one-third of the zabaglione over the cream mixture. Repeat to make two more layers.

Sift cocoa powder evenly over the top. Lightly cover with plastic wrap, being careful not to let it touch the top layer. Refrigerate for at least 4 hours or up to 3 days. To serve, cut into wedges or spoon onto dessert plates.

variation: If you like your tiramisù cakey, use 24 to 32 ladyfingers and stack them on their sides, domino style.

espresso ice cream

This creamy, rich ice cream combines the flavors of vanilla and espresso. Delicious by itself, it's also terrific in Gelato Affogato (page 87) or in Devil's Halo (page 94). I also love a softened scoop sandwiched between two Snow-Cap Cookies (page 82). Mmm — a peak experience.

makes about 1½ pints :

3 cups half-and-half

½ vanilla bean, split lengthwise

5 egg yolks

½ cup plus 2 tablespoons sugar

2 tablespoons finely ground espresso beans

method :

In a double boiler over simmering water, add the half-and-half. Scrape the seeds from the vanilla bean into the half-and-half. Cook until small bubbles appear around the edges of the pan.

Meanwhile, in a medium bowl, whisk the egg yolks and sugar together until smooth and blended, 1½ to 2 minutes. Gradually drizzle ½ cup of the hot half-and-half mixture into the yolk mixture, stirring constantly. Then gradually whisk this yolk mixture into the half-and-half mixture in the pan. Cook over simmering water, stirring constantly, until the custard thickens, about 10 minutes. To check for doneness, draw your finger through the custard on the back of the spoon; it should leave a trail. Remove from heat, and cool to room temperature.

Strain the custard through a fine-meshed sieve, stir in the ground espresso, cover, and refrigerate at least 2 hours or up to 3 days. Stir the mixture, then pour it into an ice cream maker. Freeze according to the manufacturer's instructions.

toffee-coffee crunch brittle

Chocolate-coated espresso beans and toasted
hazelnuts meet here in an irresistible coffee-
flavored candy. Broken into shards, this brittle
makes a scrumptious after-dinner tidbit with
coffee or espresso. And, if you want to make ice
cream sundaes and frosted cakes and cookies
sparkle, seal several pieces of the candy in a
plastic sandwich or storage bag, crush them
with a rolling pin or mallet, and dust them over
your dessert.

1 cup sugar

½ cup light corn syrup

¼ cup water

2 teaspoons instant coffee powder

½ cup (1 stick) unsalted butter at
room temperature

Pinch of salt

3 tablespoons chocolate-covered espresso
beans, crushed (about 22 beans)

1½ teaspoons finely ground espresso beans

¼ cup hazelnuts, toasted, skinned, and chopped
(see page 81)

½ teaspoon baking soda

method :

Generously butter a rimmed baking sheet and set aside. (I preheat the pan in a warm oven for a few minutes because the candy spreads more easily in a warm pan.)

In a 2-quart heavy saucepan, combine the sugar, corn syrup, water, instant coffee powder, butter, and salt. Cook over medium-high heat, stirring occasionally, until the butter has melted. Continue to cook to 250°F on a candy thermometer (hard-ball stage), about 15 minutes. Add the crushed espresso beans and ground espresso, and continue to cook to 280°F (soft-crack stage), 7 to 8 minutes.

Remove the mixture at once from heat, and quickly stir in the nuts, then stir in the baking soda until blended. The syrup will foam and expand. Immediately pour the syrup onto the prepared pan. With a metal spatula, spread the hot candy evenly over the pan. When cool, break the slab into pieces. Store in an airtight container—unless you eat it all first!

savories

grilled lamb chops
with coffee rub and mango salsa

Years ago, a friend from South Africa who is a coffee roaster introduced me to lamb marinated with ground coffee and spices. Now, similar highly seasoned dry rubs are showing up everywhere; they are an easy way to add a spicy crust to grilled meats. This dry rub has an ingredient to hit every taste bud: the earthy tones of the espresso bean, the sweet taste of brown sugar and ground cardamom, the peppery sharpness of ginger and chili, and the crunch of kosher salt. While I love this rub on lamb, it is also delicious on pork tenderloin, and so is the cooling and crunchy mango salsa.

Coffee Rub:

¼ cup finely ground espresso beans

2 tablespoons Kosher salt

2 tablespoons freshly ground black pepper

¼ cup firmly packed dark brown sugar

6 to 8 cloves garlic, chopped

2 to 3 teaspoons grated fresh ginger

3 to 4 teaspoons ground cardamom

Mango Salsa:

1 large mango (see note)

1 small red bell pepper, cored, seeded, and diced

1 small jalapeño chile, cored, seeded, and minced

¼ cup diced red onion

2 tablespoons minced fresh cilantro

1 to 2 tablespoons fresh lime juice

Dash of Tabasco sauce

8 loin lamb chops (4 to 5 ounces each)

(continued)

method :

To make the rub: In a medium bowl, mix the coffee, salt, pepper, brown sugar, garlic, ginger, and cardamom together.

To make the salsa: In a medium bowl, mix the mango, red bell pepper, jalapeño, red onion, cilantro, lime juice, and Tabasco together. Use now or cover and refrigerate for up to 1 day.

To prepare the lamb, arrange the chops in a baking dish and smear each chop on all sides with the rub, using your fingers. Cover and refrigerate for 4 hours or overnight.

Prepare the grill for direct grilling; the fire should be hot. Place the chops on the grill rack about 4 inches from the heat source. Grill until nicely browned, about 6 minutes per side for medium. Serve with the Mango Salsa.

Note: Choose a mango that is tender but not mushy. To dice it, cut the fruit in half by following the curve of the pit. Then score the flesh vertically and horizontally and peel back the skin.

cowboy coffee texas chili

In the never-ending search for the perfect chili recipe, I was fortunate to taste Birdie Holland's Texas Red. Birdie was the grandmother of my friend Thomas Bruner, who brought the recipe from San Antonio to Portland. With my first bite, I learned how good chili could be.

I've tempered the recipe slightly and used the deep, rich flavor of cowboy coffee to enhance its spicy richness. If you like your chili really hot, double the amount of chili powder.

Note: Since Texans consider beans an intrusion in their brimstone concoction, they leave them out.

2 cups water

¼ cup plus 2 tablespoons coarsely ground
   coffee beans

3½ cups canned low-salt full-strength beef broth

2 teaspoons red wine vinegar

1 tablespoon dried oregano

1½ tablespoons paprika

2 tablespoons chili powder, or to taste

1 tablespoon vegetable oil

1 pound mild sausage or ground pork

2 pounds coarsely ground (chili grind) lean chuck

8 ounces lean chuck, cut into ½-inch dice

1 onion, chopped

6 cloves garlic, minced

28 ounces canned crushed or diced
   tomatoes with liquid

2 tablespoons ground cumin

½ teaspoon ground coriander

½ teaspoon Tabasco sauce

Hot-from-the-oven homemade cornbread
   and ice-cold beer for serving

method :

In a small saucepan, bring the water to a boil. Turn off heat and stir in the ground coffee. Cover and let steep for 5 to 7 minutes. Strain through cheesecloth.

In a large soup pot, combine the coffee, 1¾ cups of the beef broth, the vinegar, oregano, paprika, and chili powder. Bring to a boil and reduce heat to a simmer.

Meanwhile, in a large skillet over medium heat, heat the oil and brown the sausage or pork and ground and diced chuck in batches. Using a slotted spoon, drain each batch and add to the beef broth mixture. When browning the last batch, reserve 1 tablespoon of the fat in the skillet.

In the reserved fat, sauté the onion and garlic over medium heat until the onion is trans-lucent, about 5 minutes. Add to the broth mixture. Simmer, partially covered, for 1½ hours, adding more of the remaining 1¾ cups beef broth as needed. Stir in the tomatoes and their liquid, the cumin, coriander, and Tabasco sauce. Continue to simmer for 45 minutes. Serve in bowls, with cornbread and ice-cold beer alongside.

Chili improves in the refrigerator and freezes well. Let cool completely, uncovered, before storing in the refrigerator for up to 1 week or freezing for up to 3 months.

coffee mole
with grilled zesty shrimp

Mole, a Mexican specialty, is a rich and savory sauce made with chilies, vegetables, and often ground seeds. Some versions contain semi-sweet chocolate. Recipes for the different kinds of mole are as numerous as the Mexican cooks who consider it their trademark. Originally, this pre-Columbian sauce was made by grinding the ingredients by hand. Our recipe uses a food processor, cutting the time down to minutes.

You'll find yourself using this mole as a dip for all kinds of grilled meats. It's also delicious spread on hot tortillas and sprinkled with minced green onions. And if you make it the day before and reheat the mole, it tastes even better.

serves 4 :

24 medium shrimp, shelled and deveined

1 cup beer

1 teaspoon red pepper flakes

Coffee Mole:

¾ cup strong, hot coffee

2 ancho chilies, each 3 by 2 inches, seeded and torn into pieces

1 tablespoon canola oil, plus extra oil for brushing grill rack or pan

1 small onion, chopped

3 cloves garlic, minced

¼ cup slivered almonds

¼ cup golden raisins

1 can (14 ounces) crushed tomatoes with liquid

1½ teaspoons balsamic vinegar

1 teaspoon dried oregano

1 teaspoon ground cinnamon

½ teaspoon dry cumin

Pinch of ground cloves

½ ounce semisweet chocolate, chopped

Salt to taste

1 tablespoon minced fresh herbs, such as Italian parsley or cilantro, for garnish

Ripe honeydew melon wedges for serving

1 lime, cut into 4 wedges

(continued)

method :

In a glass or ceramic mixing bowl, combine the shrimp, beer, and pepper flakes. Cover and refrigerate for at least 1 or up to 3 hours.

To make the mole: In a small bowl, combine the coffee and chilies. Let soak until the chilies are soft, about 20 minutes. In a medium sauté pan or skillet over medium heat, heat the 1 tablespoon oil and sauté the onion until translucent, about 4 minutes. Add the garlic and sauté for 30 seconds. Set aside.

In a food processor, pulse the almonds until coarsely ground. Add the raisins and process with 2 or 3 pulses. Add the chilies and their liquid, the onion mixture, the tomatoes and their liquid, the vinegar, oregano, cinnamon, cumin, and cloves. Process until semi-smooth.

Return the mole to the pan. Partially cover and simmer over medium-low heat, stirring occasionally, for 25 minutes. Add the chocolate and cook, stirring occasionally to blend and to keep the mole from scorching, for about 10 minutes. Add salt if needed. If too thick, dilute the mole with coffee, water, or chicken broth.

To grill the shrimp: Prepare an outdoor grill, or preheat the grill pan over medium-high heat for 2 minutes. Brush the grill rack or grill pan with oil. It will smoke slightly. Cook the shrimp until evenly pink, about 2 minutes on each side. To check for doneness, cut one in half. The flesh should be opaque throughout.

To serve, place 3 to 4 shrimp on each plate and sprinkle with fresh herbs. Accompany with a small bowl of warm mole, melon wedges, and a wedge of lime to squeeze on the shrimp and the melon.

yummy yams

This dish is a Thanksgiving favorite, but why wait for the big turkey dinner? The earthy flavors of yams, coffee, and cinnamon make it a delightful side dish with roasted chicken, pork tenderloin, or if my kids have a choice, grilled hamburgers.

serves 4 to 6 :

2 pounds (2 to 3) orange-fleshed garnet yams, peeled and cut into ½-inch pieces

¼ cup extra-strength brewed coffee

1 tablespoon unsalted butter

¼ cup blanched almonds, chopped

1 tablespoon plus 1 teaspoon light rum

¾ teaspoon baking powder

3 tablespoons lightly packed dark brown sugar

¼ teaspoon ground cinnamon

1 tablespoon frozen orange juice concentrate

Salt and freshly ground pepper to taste

Toasted almonds (see page 81) and fresh sage sprigs for garnish

method :

In a pot of salted boiling water, cook the yams until just tender, 15 to 20 minutes.

Remove the yams from heat, drain, and put through a ricer or place in a bowl and mash with a potato masher. Blend in the coffee, butter, almonds, rum, baking powder, brown sugar, cinnamon, orange juice concentrate, salt, and pepper. Spoon out individual servings or mound in a 4-cup soufflé dish. Garnish with toasted almonds and sage sprigs.

variations: If you're short on time, substitute a 16-ounce can of sweet potatoes. Also, walnuts or cashews can be substituted for the almonds. If you like raisins, try soaking ½ cup golden raisins in ½ cup coffee for 30 minutes, drain, and add them to the potato mixture.

resources

Here are some of the many excellent coffee sources, guides, products, and retail businesses available. Use the list as a jumping-off point for your own exploration.

books

Davids, Kenneth.
Coffee: A Guide to Buying, Brewing & Enjoying. 4th ed.
Singapore: 101 Productions, 1991.

Feller, Robyn M.
The Complete Bartender.
New York: Berkley Books, 1990.

Illy, Francesco and Ricardo.
The Book of Coffee:
A Gourmet's Guide.
New York: Abbeville Press, 1992.

Janssen, Phillip.
Espresso: Quick Reference Guide.
Seattle: Eightball Entertainments, 1998.

Kummer, Corby.
The Joy of Coffee. 2nd ed.
New York: Houghton Mifflin, 1997.

Pendergrast, Mark.
Uncommon Grounds:
The History of Coffee and
How It Transformed Our World
New York: HarperCollins, 2000.

Schapira, Joel, David, and Karl.
The Book of Coffee and Tea.
2nd ed.
New York: St. Martin's Press, 1982.

Ukers, William H.
All About Coffee, 2nd ed.
New York Tea & Coffee Trade Journal, 1935
(available through Specialty Coffee
Association of America; scaa.org)

coffee beans, products, and equipment

As a general rule, the best place to purchase your beans and equipment is from a local coffee merchant. That way, you're help-ing your community, getting more personal attention, and, if the coffee is roasted on site, fresher product. In case that's not possible, here are some other sources.

With a billion sites — and counting — on the World Wide Web, there are undoubtedly thou-sands that deal with coffee. I've listed a few of my favorites, but take some time to discover your own using your favorite search engine, or give Yahoo!, Google, Alltheweb, or AskJeeves a try.

All4Coffee

all4coffee.com

An online store offering home and commercial coffee-brewing equipment, complimentary recipes for espresso based beverages, and accessories as well as resource materials, coffee beans and coffee business consulting services. Easy to navigate, this is a handy site for checking out brands and prices.

Bodum

bodum.com

1860 Renaissance Boulevard, #201

Sturtevant, WI 53177

(414) 884-4650 or (800) 23-BODUM

This manufacturer makes a line of coffee equipment including plunger pots (French presses), vacuum pots, and frothers. The site has easy-to-follow instructions for each style of coffeemaker, plus a list of international stores and ordering information.

Caribou Coffee Company

caribou-coffee.com

615 North Third Street

Minneapolis, MN 55401

(888) 227-4268

This company sells whole-bean and ground coffees in more than 145 stores in Minnesota, Illinois, Ohio, Georgia, North Carolina, and Michigan. Its site includes store locations and home delivery of its beans.

Coffee Review

coffeereview.com

600 Townsend Street, Suite 135E

San Francisco, CA 94103

(415) 522-5380

Founded in 1997 by Kenneth Davids and Ron Walters, this excellent site evaluates a wide variety of coffees. Under the review categories there is also a section on "cause" coffees that addresses various social and environmental causes as well as sections on equipment and even one on biscotti.

Espresso Products International

anomolee.com

172 W. Pomona Avenue

Monrovia, CA 91016

(626) 359-0798

An online store offering espresso machines, coffee grinders, coffeemakers, and accessories. Easy to navigate, with pictures and information, this is a useful site for checking out brands and prices.

Green Mountain Coffee Roasters

greenmountaincoffee.com

33 Coffee Lane

P.O. Box 657

Waterbury, VT 05676

(800) 244-1395

With its large range of beans, this wholesale roaster is known for its socially responsible products and philosophy. The site fetures an extensive online store offering coffees, coffee equipment, gifts, and food.

Peet's Coffee and Tea

peets.com

1400 Park Avenue

Emeryville, CA 94608

(510) 594-2100 or (800) 999-2132

With stores in four western states, this specialty coffee company has an extensive range of fresh-roasted coffees. Its site contains valuable information, an online store for purchasing coffee beans and products, as well as an excellent coffee tasting guide. Its creative coffee selector section leads you through the full spectrum of Peet's coffees by groups such as blends, country-

Starbucks Coffee Company

starbucks.com

P.O. Box 34510

Seattle, WA 98124

(800) 782-7286

This Seattle-based company roasts and sells its coffee beans and espresso beverages along with coffee-related accessories and equipment primarily through its retail stores. Its site offers online ordering of fresh beans and accessories plus the addresses of and directions to its many retail locations.

Sweet Maria's Coffee Roastery

sweetmarias.com

9 E 2nd Avenue

Columbus, OH 43201

A terrific online store specializing in home coffee roasting supplies (at good prices), including a wide selection of green beans, as well as coffeemakers (Cona, Chemex, etc.), espresso machines, grinders, and accessories such as gold-plated filters. A delight to navigate, with good pictures, plus excellent instructions and comments for using various brewers.

general index

recipe index

table of equivalents

The exact equivalents in the following
tables have been rounded for convenience.

liquid/dry measures :

U.S.	Metric
¼ teaspoon	1.25 milliliters
½ teaspoon	2.5 milliliters
1 teaspoon	5 milliliters
1 tablespoon (3 teaspoons)	15 milliliters
1 fluid ounce (2 tablespoons)	30 milliliters
¼ cup	60 milliliters
⅓ cup	80 milliliters
½ cup	120 milliliters
1 cup	240 milliliters
1 pint (2 cups)	480 milliliters
1 quart (4 cups, 32 ounces)	960 milliliters
1 gallon (4 quarts)	3.84 liters
1 ounce (by weight)	28 grams
1 pound	454 grams
2.2 pounds	1 kilogram

length :

U.S.	Metric
⅛ inch	3 millimeters
¼ inch	6 millimeters
½ inch	12 millimeters
1 inch	2.5 centimeters

oven temperature :

Fahrenheit	Celsius	Gas
250	120	½
275	140	1
300	150	2
325	160	3
350	180	4
375	190	5
400	200	6
425	220	7
450	230	8
475	240	9
500	260	10